Arthur C. Clarke's
Chronicles of the Strange and Mysterious

Arthur C. Clarke's
CHRONICLES OF THE STRANGE AND MYSTERIOUS

John Fairley and Simon Welfare

GUILD PUBLISHING
LONDON

This edition published 1987 by
Book Club Associates
by arrangement with Wm Collins

First published in 1987
Copyright © Arthur C. Clarke, John Fairley
and Simon Welfare 1987

Photoset in Linotron Century Schoolbook by
Rowland Phototypesetting Ltd
Bury St Edmunds, Suffolk
Made and printed in Great Britain by
William Collins Sons & Co. Ltd, Glasgow

Contents

Foreword

It is now almost a decade since John Fairley, Simon Welfare and I started to assemble the extremely miscellaneous bits and pieces which eventually formed the thirteen-part Yorkshire Television series, *Arthur C. Clarke's Mysterious World*, and its sequel, *Arthur C. Clarke's World of Strange Powers*. In each case, our object was to intrigue and entertain the viewer by presenting unexplained phenomena and objects, and curiosities of any kind which we found interesting. We had no particular bias or philosophical party line, but we were determined to play fair with our audience. We would not cheat by creating phoney mysteries or withholding explanations when they were available – as has frequently been done by networks our lawyers won't allow us to mention. At the same time, we were not out to 'debunk', except when the subject richly deserved it; even then, we kept editorial comment to the minimum and preferred to leave the final decision to the viewer. And when, as sometimes happened, a mystery got deeper and deeper the more we investigated, we weren't ashamed to admit total bafflement.

The same policy was carried out in the two books based upon (and named after) the programmes. Text and video both had a very large – indeed, global – audience and, as might be expected, there was a great deal of feedback from viewers and readers. Many people rushed to report events similar to those we had recorded, or to volunteer explanations of outstanding mysteries.

Almost all the letters received were thoughtful and serious; only a few – perhaps surprisingly, considering the nature of our material – were wildly eccentric. The most far-out one arrived with a covering note headed 'Broadmoor Hospital Mental Health Act 1983', and an assurance by the consultant forensic psychiatrist that nothing had been removed from the packet. (If you're dying to know, it contained a mass of numerology no crazier than much that has been produced outside mental hospitals. The impetus that pocket calculators have now given to this age-old nonsense is appalling to contemplate.) We do not know whether to be pleased or disappointed that few clear-cut solutions or answers emerged from all this correspondence; but we are very happy to know that we made people realize that there's a lot more in the universe than meets the eye (and sometimes, a good deal *less*).

It would have been easy to make another television series – or at least one or two 'Specials' – out of the material we'd accumulated, but I had grown rather tired of standing in front of cameras in the Sri Lankan sun, even with the protection of that notorious beach-umbrella. So a book seemed the best compromise; but what to call it? My colleagues' first uninspired suggestion was *Arthur C. Clarke's Diary of the Strange and Mysterious*. This I rejected instantly as being too reminiscent of *Mrs Dale* and innumerable other soap operas. (Though

I *do* have a diary, it is for appointments only, and the entries self-destruct into total illegibility within a month.) After a little thought, I came up with an alternative which sounds much more romantic and imposing – indeed, almost heroic.

Here, then, with a little – well, frankly, rather a lot of – help from my friends John and Simon, are my *Chronicles of the Strange and Mysterious*. As many of the items chronicled end up even stranger and more mysterious than when we started to investigate them, the series could obviously go on for ever. I promise you that it won't. There's a nice symmetry about a trilogy, and I have no intention of spoiling it.

Arthur C Clarke

Colombo, Sri Lanka, 21 October 1986

1.

The Beasts that Hide
from Man

Arthur C. Clarke writes:

Would you care to guess how many kinds of unknown animals – i.e. creatures that have never been described by science – there still remain on this planet? A hundred? A thousand? The answer may well be in the millions – if you go all the way down to insects barely visible to the eye. And the vast majority never will be discovered; the accelerating destruction of the natural environment means that they will be extinct before they are even noticed.

To most people, however, an 'unknown animal' won't be of much interest unless it's at least as large as a dog – better still, an elephant – best of all, a dinosaur. Most zoologists are willing to admit that large creatures still remain undiscovered in the sea. But on *land*? Impossible, of course . . . but read on, starting with this delightful letter from Dr Dalrymple, which takes me instantly back to *Saunders of the River*:

Dear Professor Clarke,
We have been watching with great keenness your TV Programme *The Mysterious World*, and I feel that the following might be of interest to you:

In 1935, I was Medical Officer on the River Gambia in West Africa. One night, I was awakened by much noise, by the locals. The next morning, I discovered the excitement had been caused by the appearance of what they called the 'NIKENANKA'. This animal was described as 'having the face of a horse, a neck like a giraffe, a body like a crocodile, a long tail, and being about 30 ft long'. I asked the Head Men to let me know, next time this animal was seen. It was said to appear only from time to time, on moonlight nights, from the mangrove swamps where it lived, submerged in mud.

Several months passed, and, one evening, I was told of the re-appearance of the animal. However, the swarms of mosquitoes, off the swamp, were such that I turned back without seeing the 'NIKENANKA'.

As MO Rivers, I regularly visited the various stations and had occasion to call on the Manager of one of the trading Companies. During lunch, we heard a great disturbance in the nearby local market. We went out to investigate and discovered one of the manager's servants waving the educational magazine called *Animals of the World*. The excited crowd was shouting that the White Man had photographed the 'NIKENANKA': it was, in fact, a photograph of a concrete dinosaur, in one of the New York parks. They all recognized this as the animal they had seen in the swamps, on moonlight nights.

Later on, I was on board ship, travelling back to Nigeria, and a Marine Department Officer told me that, when checking the traffic lanes in the Niger Delta, his attention had been drawn by his crew to a large 'sea serpent'. He fired his gun but was out of range. The creature, however, must have heard the report, as it reared up, turned its head, and made swiftly for a mangrove swamp island. The sun was setting, and it was too dark to be absolutely certain, but he thought the animal was between thirty to forty ft long, similar to a dinosaur, as it heaved out of the water and disappeared into the mangrove swamp.

Below: Dr Thomas Hardie Dalrymple, Medical Officer for the West African Medical Service on the River Gambia.

This is, I am afraid, all I can tell you, but, as the Gambia River is about 200 miles long and the mangrove swamps, on either side, vary from 50 to 100 ft wide, it represents a large expanse of, then, unexplored ground, and I always felt there was the possibility that some animals, long thought to be extinct, might be surviving there.

Some years later, I was stationed in the British Cameroons. I became very friendly with the Fon (Chief) of N'SAW. Later, I was accepted into the two most powerful Ju-Ju societies, known as the N'FU BA and the N'FU GAM. It was then, that I was told of the existence of

'KABARANKO', said to be a human, living down a well, and existing on human excreta. He was only let out for the funerals of very important chiefs. I saw him once at such a funeral. He was said to be endowed with superhuman strength and I watched (and photographed) him pick up a ram and tear it in two. I believe he also picked up a big car and threw it over a cliff, but I did not see this.

What he was, I do not know, but he looked like a short human figure, covered in long black hair. He was greatly feared and, when brought out, he was controlled with ropes attached to his feet, one man walking in front and one at the back, in the same way farmers guide dangerous bulls. If he happened to escape, the natives whistled loudly, as a warning to everybody to keep out of 'KABARANKO's' way. The only way to recapture him was to hold a pregnant woman in front of him, when he would fall, unconscious, on the ground.

I never found out who or what he was.

Hoping the above will be of some interest to you.

Yours sincerely,
(THOMAS HARDIE DALRYMPLE)
Retired Medical Officer
West African Medical Service

The Dinosaur-Hunters

Dr Dalrymple's letter is a most evocative contribution to one of the longest-running sagas in cryptozoology – the search for dinosaurs in Africa.

The daunting, but beguiling, geography of Africa has always tempted the imagination. Dr Dalrymple describes the great stretches of mangrove swamp along the Gambia River, but there are vast stretches of swamp throughout Central Africa which remain far more remote and unexplored even than the Gambia half a century ago. The great Likouala swamps in the Congo stretch to more than 50,000 square miles. Roads are none, tracks are few, and travel is mainly by

The Upper Congo where *mokele-mbembe*
is reported to exist

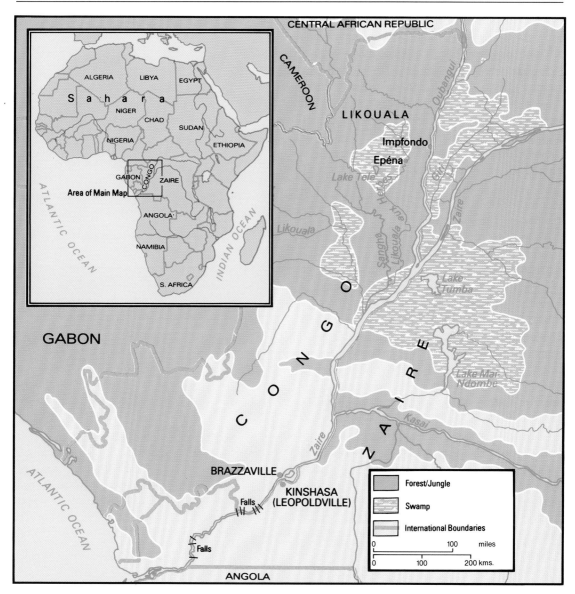

river. This area has always been the focus of speculation about the existence of huge and strange creatures unknown to science.

Immediately after the First World War Captain Lester Stevens, MC, was heading for these swamps when he was photographed, somewhat inappropriately attired and, as the *Daily Mail* caption reported, 'accompanied by his ex-German war dog Laddie, before leaving Waterloo Station for Africa to search for the Brontosaurus'. Captain Stevens was encouraged by the prospect of a $1m reward offered by the Smithsonian Institution in Washington, and by reports that two Belgian

The Greenwell-Mackal expedition up the Likouala River approaches the haunts of *mokele-mbembe*.

travellers, Gapele and Lepage, had recently seen the monster in the Congo.

Captain Stevens, though armed with a Winchester repeater, a Smith and Wesson revolver, a shotgun and a Mannlicher rifle, was sadly never to claim the reward. But his successors have not been deterred, and in recent years there have been a number of expeditions inspired by continuing reports that a great animal exists – and was even captured and killed within the last generation by the local pygmies at Lake Tele in the heart of the Likouala swamps.

Texan explorer James H. Powell, with Professor Roy Mackal of the University of Chicago, gathered the most intriguing accounts of the beast – *mokele-mbembe*, as it is known – on their expedition to the Congo in 1980. Powell had already been in the area twice before, but on this occasion the pair were able to track down a number of informants able to tell them of the killing, some twenty years earlier. Powell had a simple way of establishing with his informants exactly what animal he was seeking. He carried cards showing known animals from Central Africa, animals from other regions which would be unknown in that area, and drawings of various types of dinosaur. He would gather, by showing the cards, the local names for gorillas, okapi, etc.; check that their observations were genuine by showing, say, a bear which they could not identify; then he would show his dinosaur drawings. A number of his informants unhesitatingly identified the dinosaur as *mokele-mbembe*.

The most vivid description of the killing of *mokele-mbembe* was given to Powell and Mackal by Lateka Pascal, a fisherman who works a regular stretch of water on Lake Tele. He had heard of the incident as a child. *Mokele-mbembe* had entered Lake Tele via

Congolese biologist Marcelin Agnagna sketches the beast he sighted.

one of the waterways which drain the swamps into Lake Tele on the western side. The pygmies had blocked off this waterway by constructing a barrage of stakes and tree trunks. When *mokele-mbembe* tried to return, it was trapped by the barricade and killed with spears. According to Pascal, the pygmies cut the animal up and ate it. Everyone who ate the flesh died.

Powell and Mackal gathered together at Epena a number of people who had seen *mokele-mbembe* in recent times. One, Madongo Nicholas, described the creature – 30 ft (9 m) long or more – rising out of the water on the Minjoubou River just ahead of his boat. It had a long neck about as thick as a man's leg, the head slightly larger in diameter, and a long, pinkish-coloured back. On top of its head the creature had something which looked like a chicken's comb. Another man, Omoe Daniel, described the 8-ft (2.5-m)-wide trail left by some animal for about 100 yards as it had apparently dragged itself through the undergrowth from a pool across to the main stream of the Likouala Aux Herbes River. Another witness had seen a strange creature only half a mile or so upstream from Epena, where Powell and Mackal had convened their meeting. He identified it from a copy of *Animals of Yesterday*, which Powell was carrying, as a brontosaurus.

All those present agreed that *mokele-mbembe* lives in deep and narrow parts of the rivers, has the distinctive chicken's comb on its head – and, above all, is a dangerous animal to have seen!

The political exigencies of the People's Republic of the Congo – Africa's first Marxist state – prevented Powell and Mackal from remaining. Their visas ran out.

Mackal led another expedition the following year, but with nothing more substantial to show for another gruelling venture through mud, swamp, jungle and river. He was, however, accompanied by a professional Congolese biologist, Marcelin Agnagna, who, two years later, was to provide the latest dramatic twist in the story of the swamp dinosaur.

The 1981 expedition, which included some rigorous scientists, such as Richard Greenwell and Justin Wilkinson (both from the University of Arizona), had come to respect Agnagna's professional competence. So when, in 1983, he reported sighting *mokele-mbembe* himself, he was treated as an extremely reliable witness. Sadly, he proved to be a much less reliable cameraman.

Agnagna and a team of seven had reached Lake Tele on 1 May 1983. Agnagna himself was filming some monkeys at around 2.30 in the afternoon when there was a sudden shout. One of the local helpers called him down to the lake shore. About 300 yards away across the lake he saw an animal. It had a long back, perhaps 15 ft (4.5 m) overall, a long neck sticking out of the water and shining black in the sun, with a small head. He could see the eyes, but no other distinguishing features.

Agnagna had his movie camera in his hand, and he started to wade into the lake shallows until he was about 200 ft (60 m) from the animal. All the time he was filming. Then the animal, which had been slowly casting its head and neck from side to side, slowly submerged. The observers had had as much as a quarter of an hour to watch the creature, but no film emerged. As so often happens in the annals of cryptozoology, the pictures failed to come out. Agnagna had left his camera on a macro setting – another instance of the malign force which strikes photographers so unvaryingly when truly sensational events occur.

However, Agnagna was certain enough of his sighting. 'The animal we saw was *mokele-mbembe*. It was quite alive and it is known to many of the inhabitants of the Likouala. I saw the animal. *Mokele-mbembe* is a species of sauropod living in the Likouala swamps and rivers.' The news from Agnagna triggered a mini 'scramble for Africa', as different expeditions were mounted to try to be the first with definitive pictures and evidence. There were even accusations of 'dirty tricks', as it was alleged that the Congolese

A Royal Marine commando lies in wait for the Beast of Exmoor.

government was being lobbied to refuse visas to some and grant them to others. The perils of Congolese bureaucracy are quite sufficient in themselves, without any additional hurdles.

At the time of writing, however, no further evidence has emerged, other than of the immense difficulty of mounting expeditions to the Congo.

Puzzling Pumas, Curious Cats

The tactical situation on Exmoor in the early summer of 1983 seemed to be fully extending Britain's crack military unit, the Royal Marines. Armed with high-powered rifles and the most up-to-date night sights, the men of 42 Commando were holed up in ditches or hunkered down behind walls and hedges. From time to time a cautious sortie would be made across the rocky pastures of the Exmoor upland. The troops were frustrated: for the second time in two months they had been fruitlessly engaged. Several of them thought they had seen the target in their night sights, but each time, the quarry had been out of range.

The operation around Mr Eric Ley's farm at Drewstone had to go on, for this was the operation to hunt down the dreaded 'beast of Exmoor' – the beast that screamed in the night, displayed supernatural cunning in eluding its enemy, and was blamed for the deaths of nearly 100 sheep and lambs. A Marine officer said: 'The animal moves like soldiers themselves do, from cover to cover, and it rarely crosses open ground. It kills ruthlessly, ripping open its prey, and it can eat 35 lb of meat.'

Those Marines who had seen something flash across their night sights were convinced that the animal was a large wild mongrel dog – some latter-day Hound of the Baskervilles. Others were sceptical. Mr Ley said: 'What kind of dog is it that screams in the night? My wife has heard it and so have the troops. It is like a nightmare that never ends.'

The nightmare never has ended yet. The Marines have gone back to base, but something is still savaging the sheep and deer of Exmoor and Dartmoor, though less profligately than before.

The beast has joined the gallery of large and strange cats, dogs, lions, pumas, cheetahs and leopards reported to be running wild in Britain. Nearly 1,000 people now claim to have seen the famous Surrey puma over the last twenty years, and have gone to the trouble of telling their stories to the police. Lions have been seen in Flintshire, more pumas in Scotland, bears in Hampshire. This is the most pervasive example, in Britain, of the problem which faces the sceptical enquirer into mysteries. Can so many people, apparently intelligent and

sane, be entirely mistaken?

The Exmoor beast has some immaculate credentials. Trevor Beer, a local man and a trained naturalist, has seen it five times. Once, at close range, he saw it lope along a hedge before clearing it easily. It was dark coloured, cat-like and about 4½ ft (1.3 m) long. The most distinctive feature was the greenish-yellow eyes. Wayne Adams, aged fourteen, holidaying on Halfcombe Common, was also struck by the eyes: 'I looked over a gate and saw the animal about ten yards away. It stared straight at me with bulging greeny eyes just like a lion. It was jet black apart from white markings down its head and chest and had a head like an alsatian dog, but it was bigger than any dog we've ever seen.'

His companion, Marcus White, aged twelve, said: 'It moved like a cat but its face was like a dog's. There was no chance it was a dog. It was miles too big for that. I thought it was a panther.'

Marine John Holton saw something at 5.30 on a May morning. 'It was very big, all black and looked very powerful. It was crossing a railway line, but there was a farmhouse in the background and it wasn't safe for me to shoot.'

And so the sightings went on: school bus driver John Franks finds himself following a black beast with powerful legs and shoulders down a country lane; Mrs Doreen Lock sees it cross the road in front of her car, three miles from Drewstone Farm; taxi driver Wayne Hyde catches the beast in his headlights on Silcombe Hill: 'It had a cunning look in its eyes and very powerful shoulders.'

Game park boss Philip Lashbrook, relying on his experience in the bush in South Africa, offers to track the beast. The Torrington Foot Beagles, assisted by police with a helicopter, spend all day scouring the moor around Drewstone. But the beast eludes them all.

The Chairman of the South Molton Farmers' Union is impressed by the violence of the kills. 'This thing kills and eats lambs like no dog or fox ever did. It eats wool and all and goes for the chops. It leaves the bone structure of the neck like you would leave a fishbone.' Another local farmer reports a cow killed, 'the skull crushed by one incredible snap of the jaws'.

A beast of some description has been seen by reliable witnesses around Exmoor for at least twenty years. Police Constable John Duckworth of Tavistock saw the beast twice and collected eyewitness accounts of many other sightings. The first time he saw the animal was at Coxtorr in October 1969. He and his son had been flying a kite, but had got back into their car to warm up. Then, about 40 yards in front of them, they saw a strange animal coming towards them. 'It was about the size of a pony,' said Constable Duckworth, 'with a dog's head and ears, wolf-hound head, and a short tail. It was slatish grey with heavy shoulders and a smooth coat.' Three years later he was out shooting, also in October, about two and a half miles away from Coxtorr. The same, or a similar creature appeared, loping across some fields about 100 yards away. This time PC Duckworth had some binoculars with him and followed it until it disappeared over a wall.

Sporadic reports of sightings continued until the Great Beast Hunt of 1983. Many described the beast as more cat- than dog-like. Indeed, a landowner from Stoke Gabriel, Mr Kingsley Newman, has seen a black panther-like creature at least five times – once at close quarters behind his house after he had loosed off a shotgun at two creatures in the dark. One leapt up on to the beam of an uncompleted building. In the light of his torch Mr Newman was reportedly transfixed by the cat's blazing red eyes. The animal's coat seemed blue-black and it had a long furry tail which lashed around until the beast leapt away.

One man claimed to have shot a strange animal and buried it because he thought he might have committed some offence. Others have delayed reporting night sightings on the grounds that it might be a provocation to breathalyser custodians. There have been casts taken of awesomely large pug marks. But neither hide nor hair of the beast has fallen into the hands of its pursuers – not even a reasonable photograph. Yet still the farmers of Devon find sheep with their necks crushed, and the readers of the Devon newspapers report their close or distant encounters.

There is no doubt that there are strange animals loose in Britain. There are wallabies in Derbyshire, feral porcupines in Devon, beavers and raccoons, and probably some Arctic foxes. Many animals were released when the 1976 British Animal Act introduced much stricter controls on the keeping of large and dangerous animals. Animal societies believe that at least two black leopards were turned loose at that time. And who would have been believed if they had reported seeing a fully-grown bear on a Hebridean island? Yet Hercules the bear, famous for his television commercials, lived quite happily for two weeks on Benbecula in 1980 after escaping from his owner.

Evidence does turn up. Ted Noble, a farmer at Cannick near Loch Ness in the Scottish Highlands, repeatedly, over several months, saw his sheep savaged by what looked like a panther or leopard. His neighbour, Jessie Chisholm, had seen the animal only yards

Scottish farmer Ted Noble finally managed to trap the puma which had been savaging his sheep for several months.

away when her hens suddenly started to clamour. By the hen run was a black cat, bigger than a labrador dog, with a thick tail longer than its body. Then a visitor to Mr Noble's farm brought in the carcass of a lamb: he said he had seen it dropped by a large cat as it jumped over a deer-proof forestry fence. The head of the lamb had been almost severed and there were deep puncture wounds on both sides of the chest.

Mr Noble and his sister-in-law saw the animal several times, once even stalking one of his Shetland ponies. Finally, spurred by local derision, he constructed a trap. The bait was a sheep's head hung at the back of a disguised cage. One October morning in 1980 Mr Noble found the trap sprung. Inside was a full-grown female puma. Mr Noble's losses diminished and the puma went to the Highland Wildlife Park at Kincraig, where she lived happily for another four years. Ever since, there has been the strongest suspicion of a hoax. The puma turned out to be well fed to the point of obesity and positively friendly to humans. Yet who was hoaxing who? And where did the puma come from?

Sightings of puma-like animals have continued in the Highlands, as have rapacious killings of sheep and deer. At Dallas in Moray three very large black cats were shot which appear to be a large mutation of the Scottish wildcat. And in February 1985 another expert witness saw a strange animal in the Highlands. Mr Jimmy Milne is gamekeeper and ghillie on the Wester Elchies estate at Aberlour. Early one morning he saw an animal around 2½ ft (75 cm) tall in a field on the estate. 'It was a massive beast with a black coat,' said Mr Milne. 'I've been a gamekeeper here for forty years and I have never seen an animal like it before.'

There are vast areas with neither roads nor tracks in the Scottish Highlands, and some exotic and unexpected sights – eagles that have been trained to hawk against deer by local gamekeepers, sea eagles and polecats illicitly introduced to ancient habitats where they had long been extinct. If there is a place where a wild leopard might subsist, then it is in the great wild tracts and glens to the north and west of the Caledonian Canal.

Least likely site would be the Hackney marshes in the East End of London, yet here, just after Christmas 1980, the police were

Below: Armed police and dog-handlers scoured the East End of London for three days in search of the Hackney 'bear'.

occupied for three days hunting a wild bear. The story had all the marks of a hoax, reported as it was by a ten-year-old boy, Elliot Sanderson, and his two twelve-year-old friends, Darren Willoughby and Thomas Murray. They said they had met the bear out on the marshes and had seen it claw at trees before it made off. But the story had had a macabre prelude. Only three weeks earlier, the bodies of two bears had been found floating in the nearby River Lea. They were skinned and headless. But they were bears all the same, and had presumably been alive

and in the area not long before. There were what looked like claw marks on the trees. Then there were the footprints. Yeti-watchers know how difficult it is to draw conclusions from footprints in the snow. They melt and grow larger in the sun. However, they are also hard to fake. The Hackney bear left very distinct bear-like footprints – four-clawed and meandering across the marshes. Mounted police, dog-handlers, police with rifles, all scoured the East End of London for three days before calling the hunt off.

'Bear' paw print in the snow on Hackney marshes.

Below: Maurice Gibb of the Bee Gees saw the Surrey puma: 'This huge shape sprang across the driveway.'

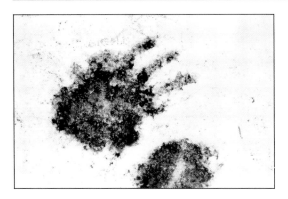

But the animal which has surely absorbed more of the British policeman's time than any other is the puma which has appeared now for more than twenty years in the back gardens, suburban roads, parks and woods of Surrey – or so many hundreds of people believe.

Policemen themselves have been among the most assertive witnesses. Back in 1963, in the early days of the puma, an animal (in this case described as a cheetah) was seen by Mr David Back. It apparently jumped right over the bonnet of a pursuing police patrol car, thus precipitating a search, fruitless, like so many that were to follow, by 126 policemen, thirty soldiers and assorted officials.

Just over the Surrey border in Hampshire, Police Constable Anthony Thomas was on patrol in Queen Elizabeth Park, Farnborough, when he had his encounter with the beast in June 1973.

It was in the early hours of the morning, but the light was good. It stood about ten yards away from me. It was three or four times the size of a cat with a long tail and pointed ears. It definitely was not a dog or a fox. There were other officers in the park with me so I radioed for help. P.C. Martin King came to my assistance, but he came up from behind the animal. As he came through the undergrowth the ani-

mal fled, but he did get a look at it. I never believed all the stories about the Surrey puma before, but I certainly believe them now.

The puma was already established in the Farnborough habitat. Mrs Heather Barber had seen it cross her path when she was cycling from the town's Queensmead shopping centre. Bricklayer John Bonnor had seen it walk from behind a pile of empty crates at the nearby Royal Aircraft Establishment in 1971. There were other sightings that year in Canterbury Road and Harbour Close.

As it hangs out amongst some of the most expensive real estate in Britain, the Surrey puma has naturally had some distinguished witnesses. Maurice Gibb of the Bee Gees pop group saw it at his home in Esher in January 1985. He said, 'We were sitting around

Photographs of the Surrey puma are few and fuzzy.

watching television, when the guard dogs suddenly tensed. I let them out and they were halfway across the lawn when they stopped dead and this huge shape sprang across the driveway and disappeared.' Mr Gibb had the large pug marks examined by experts from nearby Chessington Zoo. Their verdict was 'puma'.

Lord Chelmsford's daughter, Philippa Thesiger, came across the creature at Hazelbridge Court, near Godalming, and waved a walking stick at it to chase it away.

Mrs Christabel Arnold of Crondall, near Farnham, claims:

> I think I have been closer to this animal than anyone. I saw it face to face in Redlands Lane. I froze and we just looked at each other, then it spat all the time. It had marks like a cheetah on its face and was greyish browny beige with spots and stripes. Its back was deep red brown and massive at the back legs. It had a beautiful striped red brown and beigy white tipped tail. It had yellow slanted eyes, wire-like whiskers and tufted ears.

Mrs Arnold's neighbouring farmers also saw signs of the cat. Mr Leonard Hobbs of Marsh Farm glimpsed it once in his car headlights and often heard strange screams at night. Mr Edward Blanks found the remains of a 90-lb (40-kilo) calf which had been dragged across three fields, and then a heifer was found badly clawed.

The puma reports have waxed and waned over the years, and the animal's territory has spread over much of commuter-belt England. Mostly they refer to a black, panther-like creature, but Mrs Arnold, after her face-to-face encounter, spent some time looking at big cats in zoos, circuses or wherever they could be found, and was quite sure her animal couldn't be a puma. Her best guess was a lynx.

Again, as on Exmoor, neither hide nor hair nor convincing photograph has appeared in more than twenty years. Yet 1,000 people have surely seen something outside their normal experience. Something has been making a gory mess of a lot of livestock.

Author Di Francis, who has amassed a great deal of eyewitness evidence of sightings, believes there is a large unknown breed of British wildcat at large which has never been captured or classified, no doubt because of supernatural wiliness. The very variety of the descriptions (black and cat-like, striped, spotted, red-eyed, yellow-eyed, dog-like, tawny, huge-footed, lion-like) suggests that many different animals are involved. Pumas and lions do escape or are set free; domestic cats can grow to a daunting size, and they do go wild; any visitor to the annual Lambourn lurcher show in Berkshire knows that mongrel and cross dogs do come out in the most fearsome dimensions and colours. But it is hard to associate any of these phenomena with the skull-crushing, sheep-stealing beast which has confronted more than 1,000 of our fellow citizens with sufficient clarity and certainty to warrant an official report to the constabulary.

Throughout Britain now the observers are out, the cameras ready and the traps set in the hope that the next animal that takes the bait will prove to be a genuinely wild big cat and not just a tubby puma that doesn't eat raw meat and likes being stroked.

Tigers out of Time

In theory, the photographs overleaf are impossible. They appear to show a Tasmanian tiger digging away energetically at the roots of a tree in the south-west of Western Australia. The distinctive rigid tail and the striped haunches are remarkably clear. The

Kevin Cameron's photographs showing the tail and striped rear end of the Tasmanian tiger are analyzed in the august pages of the *New Scientist* in 1986.

photographs have a natural quality, and the attitude of the animal seems full of vigour.

Yet the Tasmanian tiger, or thylacine, the scientists claim, has not existed on the Australian mainland for at least 3,000 years. There has been no carbon-dated evidence more recent than that; the creature seems to have been unknown to the Aboriginals, and was not seen by any of the early settlers. It hung on only in Tasmania, where the question of its survival is a separate and intriguing mystery, since the last known tiger died in Hobart Zoo in 1936.

No one would be amazed if evidence emerged that tigers have survived in Tasmania. But the idea of tigers on the mainland seems absurd. Undoubtedly there were once thylacines on mainland Australia and, indeed, stories of their survival were finally corroborated in 1966 when David Lowry found the skin of a thylacine in a cave on the Mundrabilia cattle station in Western Australia. It was lying among the bones of other animals, including other thylacines, bats, snakes, rabbits, kangaroos, wombats and a Tasmanian devil. These bones were dated as thousands of years old. The thylacine, by contrast, was only partly decayed. Lowry said:

> The animal lay on its right side, with its head raised off the ground. The skin and hair were largely intact on the exposed surfaces and the characteristic dark bars were clearly visible. The soft tissue had decomposed. However the tongue and left eyeball were clearly recognizable. The tail was some twelve inches away from the rest of the body, probably moved there by rats.

Many zoologists found it difficult to believe that the corpse could have lain in such conditions in this state of preservation for thousands of years. The first crack in the wall of

44   New Scientist 24 April 1986

Tigers in Western Au

Tasmanian tigers apparently went "extinct" when the last spec New evidence suggests that some may be alive and well

Athol M. Douglas

EARLY in February 1985, Kevin Cameron, who lives at Girrawheen in Western Australia, shoved five photographs at me. He offered no comment, and his manner was almost aggressive. As I looked at the photographs, the identity of the animal in them was unmistakeable. It was about the size of a dog, with dark bars across the rump and a thick base to its tail. I realised that without doubt Kevin had found the Tasmanian tiger, or thylacine, alive in the southwest of Western Australia.

The thylacine was once common on the mainland of Australia, but is thought to have become extinct thousands of years ago, probably as a result of competition with the dingo. It remained quite plentiful on the island of Tasmania which, we believe, separated from the mainland about 12 000 years ago. From the earliest days, in the 1830s, European settlers on Tasmania tried to destroy the thylacine because it killed their sheep. By 1850 fears were expressed for its survival, but nevertheless the Tasmanian government introduced a bounty scheme in 1888. Over the following 21 years, before the last bounty was paid, 2268 animals were killed and officially accounted for.

The last known wild thylacine was captured in Tasmania in 1933. It died in Hobart Zoo in 1936. D. E. Rounsevell, the zoologist who wrote on the thylacine in *The Complete Book of Australian Mammals* (editor Ronald Strahan, Sydney: Angus & Robertson, 1983), commented: "It is ironic that the thylacine was not protected by Tasmanian law until 1936, by which time it was probably extinct." Since then, there have been many supposed sightings of the thylacine and several intensive and comprehensive searches, but no proof of its survival in Tasmania, let alone on the mainland.

Accepted scientific knowledge is thus completely against Kevin Cameron, but he has a set of five photographs taken in dense forest in the south-west of Western Australia, and some casts of the animal's footprints. The scientists may be incredulous, but I believe Cameron's finds are authentic.

Kevin Cameron is of Aboriginal descent. He takes pride in his ancestry, his bushmanship, and his knowledge of Aboriginal culture. He is intelligent, but until recently was illiterate. So he could not have learned about the thylacine in libraries. I find it inconceivable that anyone with his background could possess colour photographs of a thylacine as well as the casts and his detailed and exact knowledge of the

animal, unless I
The photogr
formerly directe
now at the Aus
He agrees with
nothing other t
The first pho

What is the thylacine

THE THYLACINE *Thylacinus cynocephalus* is a carnivorous marsupial about the size of a large dog. It stands about 60 cm high at the shoulder and measures between 100 and 130 cm from nose to tail. The tail is 50 to 60 cm long. The fur is coarse and sandy brown, with parallel dark bands across the back, increasing in width towards the rump. The head and forequarters are dog-like, the rump heavy and somewhat like a hyena. Females are slightly smaller and lighter in colour. Unlike dogs, the thylacine has five toes on the forefoot and four on the hind.

It is often referred to as the Tasmanian tiger, in reference to the stripes on its back and rump, but it is more apt to think of the animal as a marsupial wolf because its teeth, head and forequarters have a remarkably canine appearance. It is believed to hunt alone or in pairs, and, before the coming of European settlers and their livestock, probably fed on wallabies, possums, bandicoots, rodents and birds. It has been suggested that thylacines caught their prey by stealth rather than by giving chase.□

Last of the

a?

n Hobart Zoo in 1936.
on the mainland

Tracker's claim ignored

'Government is
blocking hunt
because habitat
is mining land'

ly seen a thylacine.
enuine. Dr Ronald Strahan,
onga Park Zoo in Sydney and
um, has also seen the pictures.
ey are authentic and could be
ne.
s the thylacine in the distance,

rs? The Hobart Zoo specimen

WA 'tiger' unearthed a second time

By ALEX HARRIS

Kevin Cameron's photographs were taken as he approached the thylacine. The first (above, left) shows his discarded rifle in the foreground, with the putative thylacine just visible in the centre of the picture. The other two pictures show the striped rump and thick tail clearly. Thylacines are supposed to have vanished from the mainland thousands of years ago

Kevin Cameron

A 'wildman' monkey photographed in China's
Huangshan mountains.

certainty had appeared. It then emerged that
there were people who claimed to have seen
mainland tigers, especially in South and
Western Australia around the area of the
Nullarbor Plain and in the bush that runs
away to the south-west tip of the continent.
Dr S. J. Paramanov, a scientist working at
Warrego in New South Wales, saw what he
believes was a Tasmanian tiger in 1949. A
party of five people travelling across the Nullarbor on horseback saw a thylacine, they
say, early one morning in May 1976. Mr
Huon Johnston said he clearly saw the
stripes and that his group was close enough
to distinguish the bull terrier-like head.

Ian Officer of Benger, Western Australia,
reports that there have been numerous sightings in recent times, including twenty-two
reported in one year. One witness, Mr Buck-
ingham, said that he had a very clear view
of a dog-like animal, grey-brown, with very
marked either dark brown or black trans-
verse stripes running across the rump, and
a thin tail.

But it is the 1985 photographs, taken in
February by Kevin Cameron of Girrawheen
in Western Australia, that provide the most
challenging evidence – something far more
concrete than anything that has turned up
in fifty years of searching in Tasmania itself.
Sceptics have asked why Cameron did not
get a picture of the animal bounding away;
why he did not shoot it, as he clearly had a
rifle; why the animal seems to be in exactly
the same position in the two photographs;
and there have been critical analyses from a
technical photographic point of view.

Cameron offers no comment. He is of aboriginal descent and an experienced bushman
who works with a pair of highly trained dogs.
Until recently he was illiterate. He seems
hardly equipped to perpetrate a major deceit.

And the photographs themselves are beguiling. They have a lack of artifice, and the
position of the animal seems full of natural-
ness and energy.

Athol Douglas, until recently Senior Experimental Officer at the Western Australian Museum in Perth, is convinced that the
animal is a thylacine. Dr Ronald Strahan of
the Australian Museum, and formerly Director of Sydney's Taronga Park Zoo, regards
the pictures as authentic and says that the
animal could not be anything but a thylacine.
Kevin Cameron also possesses casts which
show the distinctive pattern of the Tasmanian tiger: five toes on the forefeet and
only four on the hind.

Meanwhile, in the rough terrain of the
centre and north of Tasmania itself, expeditions continue to try to prove that the
animal survives. It is hard to credit that a
wolf-like creature the size of an alsatian,
so distinctively coloured, which carries its
young about in a pouch and is not notably
afraid of humans, could have evaded its pursuers for fifty years. Most of the tigers were
wiped out in the last years of the nineteenth
century by bounty hunters protecting sheep.
The last known killing of a wild thylacine
was in 1930. London Zoo's last specimen died
in 1931, and the last of all at Hobart in 1936.
Since then, and particularly in recent years,
there have been numerous recorded sightings – at least 100 of them of sufficient clarity
and detail to be accounted as reliable.

The distinguished zoologist Eric Guiler
has been involved in many forays to try to
locate the thylacine. He has placed electronic
surveillance equipment and night cameras
at likely spots, but without success. His
interest has been sustained by the apparent
authenticity of so many reported sightings.
In the early 1950s he managed to interview

a number of old men who had been tiger bounty hunters. One of them, H. Pearce, described seeing a female and three pups in the late 1940s – with the clear implication that he had wiped them out, as he had so many in the past. The old shepherds were unrepentant.

Another incident near the area known as the Walls of Jerusalem was described by a cattle drover. His three dogs were involved in a scuffle in the bush near his cabin. Only two came back. Next day he found the third dog dead, with its heart eaten out. He took his horse and two dogs to a nearby gully. The dogs ran under the horse and then a tiger appeared on a nearby rock.

Guiler lists dozens of modern sightings, often backed up by more than one witness or by other evidence. In 1960, by the Manuka River (near the spot where a sighting had been reported), he himself heard the strange yapping hunting noise that the thylacines made. In June 1976 there was a sighting on the Pieman River, and nearby a fresh wallaby kill. In 1981 at Mount Eliza there

were quite clear tracks of the distinctive five toes followed by four toes. Since the 1960s there have been a whole clutch of sightings at Woolnorth, which was one of the most profitable areas for the bounty hunters of the last century.

Almost annually now, well-equipped expeditions set off to try to obtain final proof that the Tasmanian tiger managed to survive the depredations of less ecologically minded generations of Tasmanians. Yet so far the nearest thing to evidence comes from Kevin Cameron's photographs, by all accounts taken far away on the Australian mainland, 2,000 or 3,000 years out of time.

The Communist Wildmen
If there are unknown 'wildmen' still to be found on this earth, the odds are that they lurk protected not only by some of the remotest landscapes on our planet, but also by the severe and daunting frontiers of the two great Communist superpowers. Details are slowly emerging of the extraordinary pro-

Below: Zhou Guoxing: his first 'wildman' theory was proved correct.

liferation of sightings and evidence now being collated by researchers in both the Soviet Union and China.

In 1985 newspapers in the West carried a colourful Reuter report from Peking, quoting the *China Daily*. It said that a 3 ft 7 in (1.1 m) tall male wildman had been caught in the mountains of Hunan and was living in a flat in the city of Wuhan. The story was soon to be retracted. But, in its resolution, it was to provide a fascinating insight into the state of 'wildman' research in China. For the creature turned out to be a previously unknown type of monkey – the very animal that had been predicted by Chinese researcher Zhou Guoxing in his analysis of wildman evidence.

Zhou, a staff member at the Peking Natural History Museum, and his colleague, Professor Wu Dingliang, Director of Anthropological Research at Shanghai's Fudan University, had both taken part in the vast Chinese Academy of Sciences expedition in 1977 to the Shennongjia Mountains. More than 100 people had been involved for nearly a year. They collected casts of footprints, pieces of hair, faeces and, most importantly, they collated the many accounts of 'wildmen' from the local people. From this evidence Zhou and Professor Wu concluded that there were two creatures involved. The first – apparently about 4 ft (1.2 m) high – was an unknown type of ape or monkey. The second – 7 ft (2.1 m) tall or more – was a large unknown species of primate, they thought.

Within five years the first part of their

Below: The hands and feet of the wildman.

theory was to be proved right; evidence for the second part accumulates rapidly.

The vast arc of virtually uninhabited territory which runs from Afghanistan along the Soviet–Chinese border, through Tien Shan and then down southern Mongolia for more than 2,000 miles, is remote to an almost unimaginable degree. Even the nomadic herdsmen make only occasional excursions into the high mountains. It can be 400 miles from one road to the next. Tibet, to the south, is, by comparison, heavily populated. Much of the area is still thick primeval forest rising up the Shaal Tau and the Altai Mountains.

It was in 1981 that Zhou first heard that there were relics of a wildman preserved in Zheijiang province. The next year he was able to make a trip to investigate. In the village of Zhuanxian he met a woman, Wang Congmei, a cowherd, who as a girl (back in May 1957) had encountered the creature. She said it had a head like a man and almost hairless skin. When it stood erect it was at least 1 m (3 ft 3 in) tall. Walking, it went on all fours, rather like a panda. The creature had been killed by Wang's mother, Xu Fudi, and a party of villagers. The local schoolmaster, Zhou Shousong, had preserved the hands and feet.

Even in their shrivelled state, the hands and feet, pictured here, presented a haunting sight. Zhou had heard similar stories before. Road builders in Xishuang Banna had killed what they called a 'wildwoman' in 1961. It had walked upright, being 4 ft (1.2 m) tall or more. They said its hands, ears, breasts and

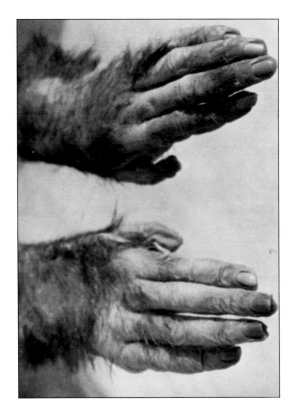

genitalia were similar to those of a female human.

Many witnesses in Yunan said that such wildmen still walked about. Zhou took careful measurements of the severed hands and feet of the Zhuanxian wildman – it had been very certainly male, Wang Congmei said. He also took plaster casts and samples of hair back to Peking. After careful analysis and consultation he concluded that the creature was neither a man nor an ape, but an unknown type of large monkey. Within a year his theory was to be justified.

In 1983 a large monkey was captured in the Huang Mountains and taken to the Hefei Zoo. It is nearly 1 m (3ft 3 in) high, has hands and feet like Wang Congmei's creature, and certainly has the strange flat finger and toenails which give such an uncanny man-like appearance to the severed hands and feet from Zhuanxian.

Then in 1985 came the second capture, at first excitedly announced as a wildman. This time the animal had been discovered in Chengbu, Hunan. It had started throwing rocks and sand at two young girls who were out in the foothills. They had run home to tell their parents, who had organized a party which succeeded in capturing the animal. Chinese researchers are now involved in attempting to classify both creatures, which certainly seem to be a new species.

The fact that local people's accounts of the small 'wildman' had been so swiftly and precisely justified, despite much academic scepticism, encouraged Zhou to pursue his analysis of the large 'wildman' sightings. These presented an altogether more fearsome picture. There have been hundreds of reports, but two in particular seemed worthy of note because they came from scientists.

Back in 1940 a biologist, Wang Tselin, had been travelling in the Gansu area. He had seen a 'wildman' killed by local hunters. He had no camera and no means of preserving or transporting the body, but his description is precise and extraordinary. The body was a female with very large breasts. It was 7 ft (2.1 m) tall and covered with grey-brown hair. Above all, Wang was struck by the primitive but human configuration of the face, which reminded him forcibly of the famous (and then newly discovered) Peking man.

Ten years later a geologist, Fan Jingquan, was out with a group of local guides in the forest near Baoji in Shangsi Province. They came across two wildmen – apparently mother and son. The description was similar. Fan was struck by how tall they were. Even the child seemed nearly 5 ft (1.5 m) tall.

In 1977 there was another spate of reports of wildmen in the mountains of Tabai in Qinling. Villagers who had encountered the creatures reported that they were 6½ ft (2 m) tall, walked upright, and were covered with hair. They left huge footprints.

Zhou and Professor Wu Dingliang are now convinced that there is an unknown large species living in the Chinese–Mongolian border area. Zhou concludes: 'I am of the opinion that it is quite possibly a descendant of Gigantopithecus which was thriving in the mainland of China in the middle and later Pleistocene period.' He points out that the panda and the orang-utan are survivors of the fauna of the Pleistocene which managed to remain in middle and western China – the panda right up to the present day. 'It is not impossible that Gigantopithecus, as the dominant member of this Pleistocene fauna, could also have changed its original habits and characteristics and survived to the present.'

Some anthropologists have even made a connection between Gigantopithecus and the famous Ice Man exhibited by showman Frank Hansen in the Minnesota area in 1968. This ape-like corpse, frozen in a block of ice, was denounded by some as a rubber fake concocted in the environs of Hollywood. Bur Dr Bernard Heuvelmans, the 'father' of cryptozoology, who examined it over three days, was convinced it was genuine – certainly a hominoid, perhaps Gigantopithecus. He believed from his inquiries that it had been shot in Vietnam during the war and smuggled back in the 'corpse bags' used by the United States Army to return the remains of their casualties. Vietnam was certainly an area where Gigantopithecus flourished.

Fittingly, twenty years on, one of the first scientific ventures between the old enemies was an investigation of Gigantopithecus at Lang Son in the north of Vietnam. Early in 1988, Russell Ciochon and John Olsen of the University of Arizona were due to start an excavation at a cave where bones have been found with a view to determining how near to modern times the great 600-lb creatures might have survived.

Russian and English anthropologists, notably Boris Porchnev and Myra Shackley, have proposed the most daring hypothesis for the 'wildmen' of Mongolia and the Altai mountains. They suggest that there may be surviving groups of Neanderthal man, who supposedly died out 30,000 years ago.

Myra Shackley, a Leicester University lecturer, made a 2,000-mile expedition to Outer Mongolia in 1979. In 1983 she published her review of the expedition. She had found a number of Neanderthal tool kits in open-air sites on the river terraces in the Altai Mountains. They included scrapers, rough chopping tools, and small flakes which had been used, then resharpened. They were made from jasper, agate and chalcedony, rocks much favoured by Neanderthals.

Myra Shackley estimated the Mongolian sites to be less than 20,000 years old. 'They may indeed be even more recent,' she says, 'since many of the tools are fresh and surprisingly unworn if they have been resting on the surface for that length of time.' She reports:

> My first line of approach was to show examples of Neanderthal tools to the people and ask whether they had seen anything like them. I obtained the same answer from a number of widely separated groups. All agreed that the tools had been used by people 'who used to live in this area before us' and who now 'live in the mountains'. The name given to these people never varied; the locals called them either the people of Tuud or, when asked to elaborate, gave them the name Almas or one of its local variations.

Shackley was convinced by the stories of the people she met. 'For me there is no question of whether the wildmen exist – I find the evidence compelling – but only of how they should be classified.'

Across the border in the Soviet Union, almost annual expeditions are taking place, concentrating particularly on the Pamir Mountains, in pursuit of the continuing reports of Almas. A member of the 1981 group, Vadim Makarov, found one of the biggest footprints ever discovered. The plaster cast shows a four-toed foot measuring over 19 in (50 cm). There were several distant sightings on this expedition, but none so vivid as the one made the previous year by an eighteen-year-old student, Nina Grineva.

She had set up camp near a sandy riverbank where she had earlier noticed foot-

'Wildman' territory along the Soviet-Chinese borders.

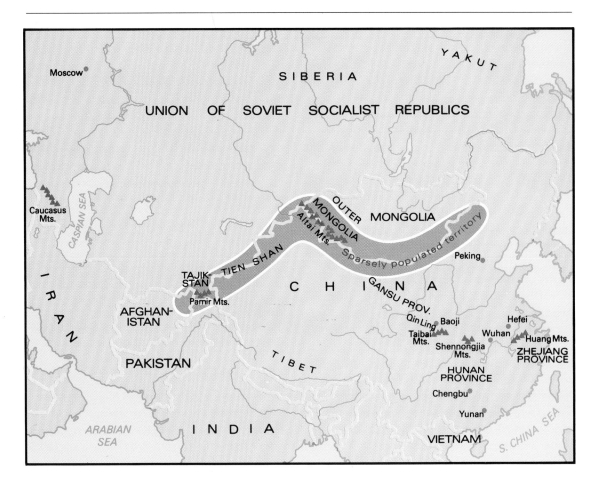

prints. She was awoken one night by the sound of stones being knocked together. 'Sixty feet away stood a very hairy person about 7 feet high. His figure was massive, almost square. He stooped and had a very short neck. His arms hung loosely. I was not scared and began slowly to advance towards him.' Nina had a toy rubber bird in her hand which she squeaked to attract the creature's attention.

> It was this that spoiled our contact [she said]. He made a sharp turn and quickly went down the slope to the river and disappeared beyond the steep bank. I noted the softness and grace of his walk, though he moved very fast. It was not a human walk, but as of an animal, as of a panther. Despite boulders and other obstacles, he moved quickly, softly and even gracefully. He must have a perfect sense of balance, and, to him, a steep and uneven slope is like a paved road to us.

The reports of these expeditions, collated by the Darwin Museum in Moscow, continue to generate controversy inside the Soviet Union. There are scattered sightings in the Caucasus, and even in the Yakut area of eastern Siberia.

The case for continuing research and exploration is championed by Dimitri Bayanov at the Darwin Museum, who points out that wildmen are prevalent in Russian and Mongol folklore and mythology. 'We say that if relic hominoids were not reflected in folklore and mythology, then their reality could truly be called into question. Of course the reality of relic hominoids cannot be supported by recourse to folklore alone. But the folklore is a valuable reinforcement of the other evidence we have.'

In 1983 Bayanov led an expedition to Tajikstan. He visited the site near Lake Pairon where two women, Geliona Siforova and Dima Sizov, had reported seeing a female wildman sitting on a boulder 10 yards (9 m) from their tent. It surveyed them for a long time, making munching sounds. They did not dare to approach it, and in the morning there were no traces of footprints or hairs.

Bayanov also visited the area of Sary Khosor and talked with Forest Service workers, who said they often had reports of wildmen. Two years previously, a shepherd had driven his sheep back down from the mountains two months early because he had seen a big black 'gul' or wildman near his pasture. It had frightened his dogs and he had not dared to stay. Another Tajik had told the officers of an encounter five years earlier with 'a giant hairy man, very broad in the shoulders, with the face like that of an ape'.

The Forest Service takes these reports seriously enough to prohibit its employees from spending the night alone in the mountains, for fear of these wildmen.

Bayanov had no personal encounter with wildmen, but he concluded his 1982 expedition report by saying:

> The abundant signs I witnessed of local fauna, particularly omnivores such as bears and wild pigs, indicate enough food resources for the presumably omnivorous hominoids the year round. The 93 percent of the Tajik Republic's territory taken up by mountains is virtually devoid of permanent human population, so the latter poses no special danger to wild hominoids. The long and continuing record of purported hominoid sightings, supported by these new accounts, leads me to the conclusion that such creatures do exist there.

However, the whole idea of wildmen regressing from Neanderthal or any other prehistoric men is anathema to Marxist–Leninist orthodoxy. Bayanov's interest and the work of the Alma expeditions were heartily denounced in 1985 by Soviet explorer Vadim Ranov. 'This hypothesis is wrong and easily refuted,' he told a meeting in Dushanbe, reminding his audience of the Marxist ideal of progress. 'We must remember that *Homo sapiens* evolved in a constant process of social as well as biological evolution.'

Clearly there are political as well as scientific hazards in the path of the enthusiastic researchers of Moscow and Peking.

The Nanjing belt. The discovery of aluminium amongst
the fragments suggested that the Chinese isolated the
metal at least 1,500 years before western scientists.

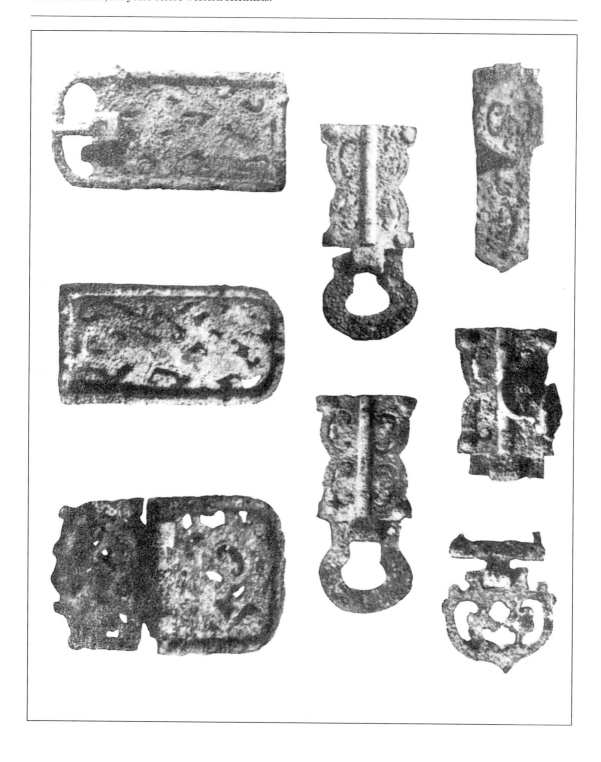

2.

The Silence of
the Past

The Nanjing Belt

The most puzzling archaeological mystery of ancient China came to light in the true tradition of buried treasure when a workman's spade broke through the roof of a long-forgotten tomb.

It was 1 December 1952. The Jingyi Middle School of Yix-ing City in the Jiang-su Province of China was building a sports field. The first task was to level the ground, for the school authorities had chosen a patch of land dominated by an oblong hillock. Another feature of the site, four curiously shaped mounds, complicated the work. That day, a labourer's shout brought everything to a halt. His spade had penetrated a thin layer of earth and rubble and a hole had appeared, releasing a rush of musty air. Peering into the darkness, the work gang could dimly make out a chamber stacked with dusty objects.

They called the police, who climbed down through the opening and soon announced that the workers had made a major archaeological find. The place was obviously a tomb. After taking into safekeeping a motley collection of grave goods, including five pieces of porcelain, eleven of pottery, some scraps of gold, two pottery stands and 'four gold articles', the police sealed the chamber and the Huadong Historical Relics Working Team was summoned to conduct a full-scale excavation.

The dig revealed that there were in fact two tombs, both built in an unusual style. Each had chambers with an arched roof constructed of wedge-shaped bricks, topped with a square slab. More bricks, laid in a herringbone pattern, covered the floor. The roof was adorned with carvings: circles, tigers or the faces of animals. Conveniently, the 'Number 1 tomb' contained an inscription which enabled the archaeologists to date their find precisely. On one side it read: '20th September of the seventh year of Yuankang the late general Zhou . . .'; on the other, the tomb builders had left their official titles and signatures: 'Yicao Zhu Xuan, jianggongli Yang Chun, workman Young Pu made.' This, then, was the burial-place of a nobleman called Zhou Chu.

Zhou could be traced in the historical records. A renowned military man and scholar, he had lived during the Jin Dynasty (AD 265 –420), and had died fighting the Tibetans in 297. There could be no doubt whatsoever about the dates, and this made one discovery all the more astonishing. Encircling what had once been the waist of a rotted skeleton found in the 'Number 1 tomb' were about twenty pieces of metal, obviously the remains of a belt. 'The factor worth noting,' wrote archaeologist Luo Zong-chen with what proved to be breathtaking understatement, 'is the chemical composition of these ornaments.' For analysis of one fragment by the Chemistry Department of nearby Nanjing University revealed that it was composed almost entirely of aluminium. Now, although aluminium is widely used in modern life, it was not isolated in the West until the early years of the nineteenth century, and a generation later was still so rare that it was a showpiece of the 1855 Paris Exposition. The production of aluminium requires something thought to have been quite unknown in ancient China: electricity. The discovery of the belt therefore raised a question which fascinated archaeologists, metallurgists and chemists both inside China and far beyond its boundaries: did the Chinese beat European scientists to the isolation of aluminium by a cool 1,500 years?

While it would be going too far to say that archaeologists have become used to pondering such problems—their working lives are usually devoted to the painstaking accumulation of more prosaic evidence of the daily lives of ancient peoples—a few objects like the Nanjing belt have presented them with an irresistible and potentially unsettling challenge. Did the scientists, artists and builders of the past know secrets that their successors have taken centuries to rediscover? Should our ideas about the level of technology achieved by the ancients be drastically revised?

How then did the experts set about findng the answer to the puzzle of the Nanjing belt? As so often happens, they first fell to arguing. In China itself the pages of the academic journals were full of the controversy. In the magazine *Koagu*, one expert, Shen Shi-ying of the North Eastern Engineering College, reported that he had carried out several methods of analysis on a small broken piece of the belt which he had obtained from the Nanjing Museum. 'But,' he announced, 'the results of these various analyses all pointed to these alloys being silver-based rather than

aluminium-based.' Another piece gave similar results, but yet another fragment, originally sent to a different analyst, really did seem to contain aluminium. Yet Shen Shiying remained sceptical and concluded: 'It is impossible to tell from its structure whether it was made in ancient times. At the same time, it was unlike the product of a 1960s factory.' He suggested that the aluminium might have been made at the beginning of this century, but added cautiously, 'This is only a supposition, and to know definitely, all round research in depth is called for.'

Stung by Shen's reservations, and particularly by his suggestion that the piece of metal which analysis *had* proved to be aluminium had been introduced into the tomb at a much later date, perhaps by grave-robbers (who had undoubtedly broken into the tomb at some time in the past), one of the original excavators, Luo Zong-chen, published a riposte. The belt pieces, he wrote, were certainly of the Jin period, for most of them 'were underneath the accumulated earth, showing that they had never been disturbed'. Luo also attacked Shen's assertion that most of the fragments found had turned out to be silver. Four pieces, he conceded, had indeed been shown to be silver, but four others *were* made of aluminium.

The Cultural Revolution of the 1960s, which so disrupted Chinese academic life, brought the controversy to an abrupt end with nothing resolved, but by then the story was out. One of the many experts in the West who learned of the Nanjing belt was Dr Joseph Needham of Cambridge University, author of the monumental *Science and Civilisation in China*, and perhaps the greatest authority of all. He was intrigued and did not entirely dismiss the idea that the ancient Chinese had somehow found a way to isolate aluminium. 'For the present it would be un-wise to rule out the possibility,' he wrote in 1974.

One group of Western scientists, however, did not stop at simply expressing interest in the Nanjing belt. In 1980, inspired by Joseph Needham, Dr Anthony R. Butler and his colleagues, Dr Christopher Glidewell and Sharee E. Pritchard, of the Chemistry De-partment of the University of St Andrews decided to continue the search for the truth, begun a quarter of a century earlier in China. In 1986 their report was published, and was eagerly consulted by scientists and lay people whose curiosity had been whetted by the Chinese controversy. Its title, 'Aluminium Objects from a Jin Dynasty Tomb – Can They Be Authentic?' held out the promise that the three investigators had found an answer to the mystery.

They began by acknowledging that mod-ern research into Chinese science and tech-nology has revealed many previously unsuspected scientific and technological achievements, some astonishingly advanced. 'Consequently we believe that no report of a medieval Chinese chemical achievement, however remarkable, should be rejected without adequate modern re-assessment.' Even so, they judged that the production of aluminium in the Jin Dynasty, an age without electricity, 'would have been truly remarkable'. The St Andrews researchers then went on to pose questions which many had asked but none had proved able to answer: 'How reliable is the archaeological evidence? How reliable are the chemical analyses? What metallurgical techniques were available at that date? Is it possible to prepare an aluminium alloy by any of them? If an aluminium alloy was prepared, was it by design or by accident?'

Their discussion of the archaeological evi-dence did not detain them for long. They argued that standards of excavation are high in China—the painstaking manner in which the first emperor's terracotta army has been uncovered and preserved at Xian is one of the most recent examples—and concluded that 'there can be little doubt that the alu-minium artefacts were found in the tomb'. They also gave short shrift to a suggestion that the belt had somehow been 'planted' by grave-robbers:

> It is difficult to see why they should have left the silver objects in place and have carefully inserted pieces of aluminium for the confusion of future excavators. A tomb-robber is scarcely likely to have had scraps of kitchen utensils about his person and to have discarded them accidentally. It would also need a miraculous breeze to replace the dust.

Butler and his colleagues devoted most of their paper to the central question: Did the Chinese of the Jin Dynasty have the know-how to produce aluminium? While the mod-ern method of isolation uses electricity, aluminium has been produced in furnaces, though these need to be extremely hot. The Chinese certainly had furnaces capable of producing high temperatures, perhaps as great as 1,500°C, but, the St Andrews team concluded, these would have been capable of making metal containing only very small amounts of aluminium. And there was no method available to Jin Dynasty metallur-gists which would have enabled them to manufacture aluminium of the purity of the metal found in Zhou Chu's tomb.

So what is the answer? How can it be that pieces of almost pure aluminium should turn up in an ancient tomb? With a touch of the theatrical, the Scottish researchers saved their theory for the last paragraph of their report:

We are led to suggest, for want of something better, [they wrote] that the aluminium was introduced as an academic prank by a participant who was probably greatly embarrassed when he realized the consequences of his actions. Fortunately for scholars in the West, the Chinese themselves were the first to doubt the authenticity of the claims. It is perhaps a mark of our regard for the enduring genius of the Chinese people that the claims were taken seriously for so long.

The St Andrews paper seemed to have settled the argument. Hoaxes, of course, are nothing new in archaeology, and the story of the Nanjing belt was duly dubbed 'the Chinese Piltdown' after the most celebrated hoax of modern times, in which a weird amalgam of a human cranium and an orangutan's jawbone, unearthed in the south of England in 1912, was successfully passed off for some forty years as the skull of an important 'missing link' in the evolutionary chain.

Yet in 1985 the *Bulletin of the Chinese Academy of Geological Sciences* reported a discovery which revived the possibility that aluminium had been available in China at the time of General Zhou's burial. Geologists from the Shenyang Institute of Geology announced that they had found grains of 'native aluminium' in Guizhou Province. 'Native aluminium' is extremely rare, indeed only a handful of claims for its discovery have ever been made. According to the Chinese geologists, their specimens contained 'some copper and sulphur, also chromium and iron' and were harder than pure aluminium, but they were satisfied that they had been found 'in a situation where contamination by men was eliminated'.

The report brought this comment from Dr Anthony R. Butler of the St Andrews team:

I think the evidence for the presence of native aluminium is good but the manner of its production is obscure. The grain size indicates that it could not possibly have been used to make the Nanjing belt. For native aluminium to have been used for that, an even rarer geological process, giving lumps of aluminium rather than grains, would be necessary. While this is a possibility, made more possible by the discovery of grains of native aluminium, it remains a remote hypothesis. However, a general rule is never to underestimate the Chinese. After all, they did invent the compass, printing and gunpowder.

The Stone 'Doughnuts'

The achievements of the ancient Chinese were also much discussed in the course of a controversy that arose after the discovery of mysterious artefacts off the coast of southern California.

In 1973 a US Geological Survey ship dredged up a peculiar stone from 13,000 ft (4,000 m) down on the bed of the Pacific, off Point Conception. Roland von Huene, the geologist who first examined it, soon noticed something odd: the stone had a hole in the middle, and 'had clearly been made by tools'. The underwater 'doughnut' was covered with manganese deposits, which suggested that it had been on the ocean floor for some considerable time.

The 'doughnut' was quite a curiosity and when, two years later, a whole hoard of similarly worked stones was located off the same coast, historians of the sea really began to get excited. Two professional divers, Wayne Baldwin and Bob Meistrell, had been exploring a reef off the Palos Verdes peninsula when they saw at least twenty stones lying 16 ft (5 m) down amidst the seaweed. They

Below: One of the doughnut-shaped anchor stones found off the Palos Verdes peninsula, California. Evidence, some theorists believe, that Chinese explorers reached America 1,000 years before Columbus.

brought a few to the surface and stored them in a yard outside a diving shop at Redondo Beach, south of Los Angeles.

The discovery of a few old stones does not often make the headlines, but the theories advanced to explain the purpose and presence of these 'doughnuts' off the Californian coast became big news. The stones, the theorists argued, were ancient ships' anchors of a type often found in the Mediterranean Sea. Sailors used to bore a hole in a heavy rock, tie a rope through it and cast this primitive anchor overboard when they wanted to moor their vessel. But it was the explanation ad-

vanced by a group of Californian academics, that sent the reporters rushing to their typewriters.

The stones, they opined, were anchors lost from Chinese ships which had visited America 1,000 years or more before—centuries before Columbus. James R. Moriarty III and Larry Pierson expressed little doubt. 'Stylistic comparisons with historical, archaeological and ethnological data indicate great antiquity for the anchors,' they wrote. 'Geologic studies show that the stone from which they were made is not of Californian origin. . . . It seems clear to us that Asiatic

Professor Frank J. Frost (*centre*) examines the Chinese
anchors with two of his students.

vessels reached the New World in pre-Columbian times.'

The idea that ancient seafarers reached America before Columbus is nothing new. Claims that the Chinese got there first rest on an account in a history of the Liang Dynasty, which flourished from AD 502 to 557. In 502 a monk called Huishen appeared at the court of the Emperor Wu Ti and told of a journey he had made to a wonderful country called Fusang. According to the mariner monk, it lay 20,000 *li* (6,500 miles) to the east of China. Some later scholars, particularly those of the mid-nineteenth century, discovered in Huishen's narrative what they took to be uncanny similarities between Fu-

sang and America, and on this somewhat slender evidence the idea that the Chinese had sailed in their junks to the New World took hold. It even survived a thorough debunking by Gustaaf Schlegel of the University of Leiden, Holland, in 1892. Schlegel argued that since Huishen's story clearly exaggerated some of the marvels he had seen – he had told of mulberry trees thousands of feet tall and of silkworms 7 ft (2 m) long – his estimates of the distance he had travelled to reach Fusang might well be inaccurate too. From his description of the features of the country, Schlegel deduced that the fabulous Fusang had really existed, but was much closer to China than Huishen had admitted.

Schlegel identified it as a large island near Japan called Sakhalin.

The discovery of the 'Chinese anchors' off California, however, revived the diffusionist arguments. In 1980 support for the American theorists who believed the anchors were evidence of a pre-Columbian landfall off California came from China itself – in the form of an article written by a leading maritime historian, Fang Zhongpu. According to Fang, 'many Chinese historians believe that the Fusang the monk Huishen had visited is today's Mexico', and he welcomed what he deemed to be this proof of 'friendly intercourse between China and America in ancient times', and argued that Chinese junks and seamen of 1,500 years ago were well capable of crossing the Pacific.

Meanwhile, however, analysis of the Palos Verdes stones by the Geology Department of the University of California at Santa Barbara, dealt a blow to the diffusionists' claims. The analysts found that the stones had not originated in China, but had come from the local Monterey shale.

Professor Frank J. Frost of the same university had been sceptical of the claims made for the Chinese, and he seized on the geologists' report in a bid to clear up the mystery.

> Presumably someone already in California shaped these stones and drilled holes in them. Both the large number of objects (about 20) and the wide distribution over more than an acre of ocean bottom would seem to rule out any conceivable pattern left by a shipwreck. Instead, the impression left is of an area where boats anchored frequently and occasionally lost their anchors. The question remains, therefore, what frequent visitors came to this reef and anchored using primitive weight anchors made of local stone?

Frost soon found an answer: the Chinese. Not the early Chinese, however, but immigrants from the Pearl River delta who had settled in California in the nineteenth century and had started a flourishing fishing industry. They had brought with them the technology of their native land, and sailed the California coast in traditional junks and sampans. To moor their vessels, they probably used the same kind of anchors as their forefathers – stones with holes bored in them. 'It is hard to resist the working hypothesis that the Palos Verdes stones represent evidence of nineteenth-century California Chinese fishermen who made frequent visits to a reef rich in marine life,' wrote Frost. He added: 'There is no other human agency in the history of the California coast that had both a need for implements made of local stone and the means to get them where they are found today.'

Professor Frost's arguments are rational and convincing, but can they be said to solve the 'Chinese anchor mystery' once and for all? There can, of course, be no definitive answer. The methods of the Chinese fishermen of California died with them and, as Professor Frost observes, 'unfortunately, a hundred years ago other Californians were more interested in driving the Chinese fishermen out of business than in studying their technology'. There is still a remote possibility that Chinese mariners *did* visit America before Columbus and fashioned anchors out of local stone, but if a mystery can be explained simply, it is perverse to settle for any more outlandish solution.

The Nazca Lines

The Nazca lines of Peru offer a more profound challenge to archaeologists, but recent research in laboratory and desert has brought a new understanding of their purpose. Theories that the lines were runways for alien

The 'giant scratchpad' of Nazca: lines, geometrical figures and drawings meticulously inscribed on the desert.

spacecraft or tracks laid out for pre-Columbian athletics meetings have long been laughed out of court.

Anthony F. Aveni, Professor of Astronomy and Anthropology at Colgate University in the United States, led a team which began an elaborate survey of the lines in 1977. Earlier, he and a colleague had studied the extraordinary *ceque* system of the Inca capital, Cuzco. This was a network of forty-one 'invisible lines' radiating out of the city. Each was punctuated at intervals by a *huaca*, or sacred place. Unlike the lines, these *huacas* actually existed, and the investigators found that many of those at the end of the *ceques* marked places near which water could be found. The system also operated as a gigantic agricultural calendar: each *huaca* signified a different day in the farmer's year, and some *ceques* pinpointed where the sun would be on important dates, thus signifying when, for example, the crops should be sown. The *ceques* were also used as ritual paths by pilgrims.

The Nazca lines were probably laid out 1,000 years before Cuzco was built. Were they, Aveni wondered, forerunners of the *ceque* system? To find out, six expeditions laboured under the desert sun; volunteers followed the lines for miles across the pampa; aerial photographers produced a photomosaic; and the triangles, trapezoids and spirals were meticulously measured. The results were fascinating. Like the spokes of a vast wheel, many lines radiated from centres, each of which took the form of a natural hill or a mound on which a rock cairn had been constructed. These centres reminded the investigators of the *huacas* of Cuzco.

Many of the Nazca lines, like their invisible counterparts at Cuzco, turned out to be associated with water. Some opened up into vast trapezoids, two thirds of which were aligned with water courses with their 'thin ends' pointing upstream. The astronomical studies added extra weight to the theory. The lines that intersected the part of the horizon through which the sun travelled in the course of the year tended to cluster around one particular area – the region where the sun appears in late October, a time especially important to the Nazca farmers, for this is when the dried-up rivers flow again with water. This suggests that the Nazca lines, like the *ceque* system, formed a giant agricultural calendar.

The survey also revealed that the lines had been used as pathways and established that they have many of the characteristics of the old Inca roads. Aveni speculated that workers might have used them to travel from one river valley to another and that the paths might have had some sort of ritual use.

This is how Professor Aveni summed up his findings:

> To be sure, our argument has proceeded by analogy, but whatever the final answer may be to the mystery of the Nazca lines, this much is certain: the pampa is not a confused and meaningless maze of lines, and it was no more intended to be viewed from the air than an Iowa wheatfield. The lines and line centers give evidence of a great deal of order, and the well-entrenched concept of radiality offers affinities between the *ceque* system of Cuzco and the lines on the pampa. All the clues point to a ritual scheme involving water, irrigation and planting; but as we might expect of these ancient cultures, elements of astronomy and calendar were also evident.

Although the question of why the lines were built is the major mystery of Nazca, there is another intriguing enigma still to be resolved: How did the Indians of at least

The 440-ft (135-m)-long Nazca condor. Until recently,
the techniques used by the Indians 1,000 years ago to
draw it were a mystery.

1,000 years ago draw the birds, insects, and animals that make up the huge 'picture book' of Nazca? The outlines are difficult to make out on the desert floor, yet from the air their precision is flawless.

In August 1982, a small group of enthusiasts assembled at a location far to the north of the 'giant scratchpad', a landfill site near West Liberty, Kentucky. Joe Nickell of the University of Kentucky, an experienced investigator of mysteries, planned to work out how the vast drawings of birds, insects and animals that probably predate the larger Nazca lines were actually inscribed onto the desert. Maria Reiche, the stalwart investigator whose study of Nazca began in the 1940s, had noticed an important clue in the course of her painstaking mapping. The draughtsmen of ancient times had made small-scale preliminary drawings of the figures on plots 6 ft (2 m) square. They had then enlarged them, section by section. There can be no doubt that this was the method used: like the lines and figures, these sketches have survived the centuries and can still be seen.

Maria Reiche was less specific about how the drawings were scaled up, however. She suggested that the Nazca Indians could have used a rope and stakes to make straight lines and circles, but was vague about how they could have found the right positions for the stakes that served as the centres of circles or the ends of straight lines. Joe Nickell thought he might have the answer, and called in two of his cousins to put his theory to the test. They decided to try to reproduce one of the most striking of the Nazca drawings, the giant 440-ft (135-m)-long condor. Nickell wrote afterwards:

> The method we chose was quite simple. We would establish a center line and locate points

Joe Nickell's condor drawn on a Kentucky landfill site
using methods and materials available to the Nazca
Indians. Nickell (*opposite*) calls it 'possibly the world's
largest art reproduction'.

on the drawing by plotting their coordinates. That is, on the small drawing we would measure along the center line from one end (the bird's beak) to a point on the line directly opposite the point to be plotted (say a wing tip). Then we would measure the distance from the center line to the desired point. A given number of units on the small drawing would require the same number of units – larger units – on the large drawing.

Maria Reiche had suggested that the desert artists had used a standard unit of measurement known as the 'Nazca foot' – about 32 cm (12.68 in) long. So, using the 'Nazca foot', a wooden T-square to ensure each measurement they made would be at right angles to the centre line, a supply of tennis-court marker-lime for drawing the outline, and with an aeroplane standing by for aerial photography, Nickell and his group (which now included his father) set to work.

The task took nine laborious hours of plotting and pegging. Over a mile of string connected the stakes, but the outline was unmistakable. After a week's delay, due to rain, they traced it out with lime, and the figure, 'possibly the world's largest art reproduction', could be photographed in all its glory from the air.

Cheerfully, Nickell summed up. They had proved that

the drawings could have been produced by a simple method requiring only materials available to South American Indians centuries ago. The Nazcas probably used a simplified form of this method, with perhaps a significant amount of the work being done freehand. There is no evidence that extra-terrestrials were involved; but, if they were, one can only conclude that they seem to have used sticks and cord just as the Indians did.

Masterpiece and mystery: the Inca sun temple at Pisac,
Peru. How did its builders manage to fit the stone
blocks so tightly together?

The Peruvian Stone Walls

Professor Jean-Pierre Protzen, Chairman of the Department of Architecture at the University of California at Berkeley, also found that practical experimentation can help solve some mysteries. While on a visit to central Peru in 1979, he became fascinated by the ruins of buildings constructed by the ninth emperor of the Incas. The huge blocks of stone, some weighing well over 100 tons, were put together in a most remarkable way: each block fitted together so tightly that it was impossible in many cases even to slide a knife-blade into the joints. What was the secret of the Inca stonemasonry? Professor Protzen assumed that when he returned to Berkeley he would be able to find out from a book in the university library. But there was no book, and no one seemed to know the answer.

In 1982 the professor set out for Peru once more, determined to crack the mystery. First he examined the spectacular Inca walls at Cuzco, Saqsaywaman and Ollantaytambo. Then he visited the quarries from which the stones had been cut, marvelling in passing at the slides down which the blocks were transported from the rockface. One slide, at Kachiqhata, had 'an awesome 40-degree slope with a 250-meter vertical drop'. At another quarry Protzen found 250 large stones which, he realized, were 'examples of all the stages of production, from raw stone to finely dressed blocks'. Scattered amongst them were stones which had obviously come from outside the quarry, probably from the banks of the Vilcanota River nearby. These, he decided, were hammers with which the blocks had been worked. He identified three types: the heaviest probably shaped the stones immediately after they had been cut from the main rockface; the medium-sized

Inca stonework at Hatunrumiyoc, Cuzco, Peru. Not even a knifeblade can penetrate the joints between the huge blocks.

ones could have been used for dressing the blocks; and the edges would have been fashioned with the smallest hammers.

The time for theorizing was over. The professor chose a likely looking block and set to. With just six blows of a 9 lb (4 kilo) stone hammer, he shaped a rough block, and then, with another hammer, pounded one of its faces until it was smooth. To protect it from the impact of heavy blows to the next face, he used one of the smallest stones to draft the edges before turning the block over. Ninety minutes later, three sides were dressed. A comparison of the test block with those worked by the Incas confirmed that Professor Protzen's hypothesis was plausible.

Now it was time to tackle the heart of the mystery. How had the Inca stonemasons managed to make the blocks fit together so tightly? The examination of ruined walls provided the clues. Joints – usually concave depressions – were cut in the lower blocks so that the upper course could fit into them precisely. The sides of each block were slotted together in the same way. Once again, Professor Protzen tried the technique himself. He took the block he had already dressed and placed it on top of another. Then he traced the outline of the upper stone upon the lower, removed the top block, and pounded away until he had hollowed out a depression for the top one to fit into. Before long, both stones were tightly locked together.

The enigmas of Inca stonemasonry had yielded to an enquiring mind and an energetic arm.

The Great Glass Slab of Galilee

There are some mysteries, however, which cannot be explained by experiment or enterprise; when archaeologists have to make do with excavation and informed guesswork. In the 1950s the local authorities near Haifa, Israel, decided to build a museum in a cave at Beth She'arim, the site of an ancient city where Jews were buried in catacombs. The cave had been used as a water tank and, since it was badly silted-up, a bulldozer was brought in to clear it. In the middle of the floor, the machine struck a large slab, which the museum administrators decided to keep and use as the base of a display case. For years afterwards, visitors filed past, looking only at the model of a building laid out upon it, not realizing that the slab itself was by far the most interesting exhibit of all.

Eventually, some local archaeologists took a closer look at the slab. To their amazement, they found it was not made of rock at all, but of strange purplish-green glass. A search through the record books brought a further surprise. The slab measured 3.40 m by 1.94 m (over 10 ft by 6 ft), was about 50 cm (nearly 20 in) thick, and weighed about 8.8 tons. This made it the third largest piece of glass ever known to have been made by man, ranking only after two giant mirrors manufactured in 1934 – making full use of the current technology – for the Hale Telescope at Mount Palomar in the United States. Yet from what was known of the history of the cave, the 'Great Glass Slab of Galilee', as it came to be called, was well over 1,000 years old.

In 1964, soon after its discovery, a team of American experts was called in to investigate the slab. Its leader, Dr Robert Brill, Administrator of Scientific Research at the Corning Museum of Glass, New York, was mystified. The slab was certainly made of glass – laboratory tests on a core taken from it with a power-drill proved as much. But what was the third largest piece of glass in the world doing in a cave in Galilee? And who had made it, and when and why? To

The Great Glass Slab of Galilee. For years this astonishing example of ancient technology went unnoticed, serving as a stand for a museum display case.

produce a slab that size would certainly have been a daunting task, requiring around 11 tons of raw material kept at a temperature of 1150°C for several days.

In fact, finding out how the glass had been made did not prove difficult. Brill and his colleagues managed to excavate beneath the slab, and there they found a layer of large stones which appeared to have once been covered with clay. This, Brill guessed, was the bottom of a large tank in which the glass must have been mixed and fired. He went on to suggest that firing chambers were probably built at the side to provide heat for melting the material and that the whole tank was covered over. He later learned from the archaeologists that, within living memory, a course of large stones had existed around the slab, and this strengthened his conviction that a tank had been used.

It was fairly simple, too, to guess why the slab had been left in the cave: Brill's chemical analysis of the core showed that it had gone wrong in the furnace. At the bottom the raw materials had not fused together properly, the whole thing had crystallized – and its dull appearance meant that no one recognized it as glass when the museum was opened.

Comparisons with other ancient glass from the area – in addition to his knowledge of the history of the cave – enabled Brill to estimate that the slab had been made at some time between the fourth and early seventh centuries, but he was at a loss to explain *why*

Dr Robert Brill excavates beneath the slab. He established that it is one of the largest pieces of glass ever known to have been made by man.

the glassworkers of ancient Galilee had embarked upon their laborious task in the first place. There was one clue, but it told him little. Manganese had been added to the mixture to give the glass its purplish colour, suggesting that it had been designed to be decorative. Perhaps, Brill speculated, the slab had been destined to be broken up into small pieces and sent out to craftsmen in other villages, who would then have fashioned glass objects of their own from them. Or perhaps the intention had been to keep it in one piece and use it in a building as an impressive architectural feature. Robert Brill was doubtful that the answer would ever be forthcoming. He wrote:

> We must in the meantime commend its unknown makers for their engineering skill. They brought over eleven tons of raw materials to a temperature in excess of 1000°C for several days, and produced a glassy consolidated mass. This was a considerable technological feat, and I know of no similar accomplishment in the metallurgical or other pyrotechnic arts in ancient times.

Dr Brill's approach is realistic. There can be no definitive solutions to such mysteries, for, as far as we can tell, the ideas and technological secrets of so many ancient civilizations were not written down. The fact that the Californian Chinese anchors were thought mysterious shows how quickly know-how can be forgotten. Scientists can learn much about mysterious artefacts by experiment, the archaeologist's spade can turn up many clues, but the exact intentions and methods of the people who traced out the huge pictures on the Nazca desert, of the Galilean glassmakers, the Inca builders and the metalworkers who worked a Chinese warlord's belt are likely to stay lost forever in the tantalizing silence of the past.

Arthur C. Clarke comments:

I am happy to see *a* solution to the mystery of the 'ancient' Chinese aluminium belt, which has worried me for years. Technologically, such an artefact would be almost as anomalous as a medieval transistor radio. Of course, the solution may not be right, but it is highly plausible – and one possible solution is infinitely better than none. Recent scandals have shown that archaeological (and other scientific) frauds are by no means uncommon, and may begin as practical jokes that sometimes get out of hand. The classic case is that of the eighteenth-century German professor whose academic rivals carved amazing fake fossils for him to discover. The fact that some of them appeared to be of fiery comets, stars

Below: William Jenna's 'ancient steamroller'. Museum experts say it is 1,700 years old, but is its resemblance to modern machinery more than coincidence?

and spiders spinning webs only increased his eagerness to publish his findings. By the time he discovered that he had been hoaxed, it was too late – and he spent the rest of his life (and fortune) buying up the volumes in which he had printed his revolutionary conclusions.

A few months ago I received a letter and photograph from Mr William W. Jenna of Bel Air, Maryland, containing information about an item which one might suspect of having a similar origin. Note that it was found on the high plateau near Nazca – where, as we have seen, some surprisingly ingenious technology once flourished!

About ten years ago, my wife and I purchased a piece of pre-Columbian pottery from a collector who had unearthed it in a dig in Peru in the late 1950s. The piece was a product of the Vicus culture, which flourished in Peru between the first and fifth century A D. Because of the location in which the piece was found, the high plateau near Nazca, it was dated by museum experts at around A D 200; at least 1,500 years before the dawn of the industrial revolution. Yet it would appear to be an exact representation of a modern steamroller, complete with a front 'smoke-stack' and, even more startling,

a cab with a driver inside, tire-treads, and wheel spokes. All this from a culture which, as far as we know, did not even make use of the wheel. Everything was carried or dragged from place to place, and it was not until the Spanish explorers conquered the area that wheeled vehicles (carts, etc.) were introduced.

Up to this point, only a handful of people have seen the piece, primarily museum curators, who, like ourselves, were both puzzled and fascinated by the piece. The thing is in mint condition, having fortunately been perfectly preserved by the extremely arid conditions of the high plateau; all the museum people agreed that it was a superb example of the Vicus double-vessel work, and all placed the date between A D 100 and 300.

The resemblance to a modern (well, 1930-ish) steamroller is certainly striking. But need it be more than coincidence? I'm prepared to admit that the makers of the Nazca lines had hot-air balloons, as has been ingeniously argued. But not steam engines.

The origin – and method of manufacture – of the stone 'Giant Balls' of Costa Rica (see *Arthur C. Clarke's Mysterious World*, Chapter 3) is still an archaeological enigma. Surprisingly, it turns out that nature *can* make almost perfect spheres of stone. Hundreds of specimens of up to 11 ft (3 m) in diameter have been found in Mexico. They appear to be of volcanic origin, and were formed some forty million years ago when a torrent of incandescent ash cooled and crystallized. Although many of these natural spheres are almost geometrically perfect, they lack the finish of the man-made ones – though James Randi has suggested that they may have inspired their production. And, one might add, greatly assisted it: any sensible sculptor starts with a piece of rock as near as possible to the shape he's aiming at.

I am indebted to my old friend Colin Ross

Below: One of the 'Giant Balls' of Costa Rica. Was it
sculpted by nature or the ancients?

for information about much smaller spheres
(the 'Moeraki Boulders') which occur in New
Zealand. These are concretions, i.e. masses
that have 'grown' from the surrounding rock
by chemical precipitation over immense
periods of time. Some are up to 6 ft (2 m) in
diameter, and range from perfect spheres to
'highly irregular and fantastic shapes'.

Natural spheres can also be produced when
rocks are trapped in holes on the beds of

rivers, and strong currents continually turn
them over and over. I am grateful to Rubert
Siemerling for this information; he tells me
that farmers in the Alps used this method to
make stone cannon balls, so the process must
be fairly swift.

Never underrate Mother Nature. In this
case, she has come up with *several* solutions
to a problem which at first sight seems
insoluble.

'They were *that* big.' Eyewitnesses to the Marksville
fish fall: Mrs Elmire Roy, Bob Neitzel, Mrs Eddie
Gremillion, Sheriff 'Potch' Didier and Anthony Roy,
Jnr.

3.

Out of the Blue

Frogs that Fly and Fish that Rain

In Marksville, Louisiana, they still remember the day J. Numa Damiens burst into the offices of the local paper brandishing a fish. The date was 23 October 1947. J. Numa had telephoned the office a few minutes before, and was incensed at the scepticism shown by the hard-bitten smalltown journalists on the *Weekly News* to his extraordinary tale.

The fish, he claimed, had fallen from the sky. It was just one of hundreds which had rained down from out of the blue. They were all over Main Street, in the yard of the director of the Marksville Bank, in Mrs J. W. Joffrion's property next door, on rooftops everywhere. Three of the town's most eminent citizens had even been struck by cascading fish as they walked to work. The morning rush-hour had been thrown into chaos: cars and trucks were skidding on a carpet of slithery scales.

The journalists heard their visitor out as he waved the fish in front of their faces, crying, 'Here's one of 'em; take a look and then see if you think I'm talking through my hat.' It certainly sounded very strange, but surely fish couldn't really have rained from the sky. Not on peaceful little Marksville, Louisiana. With their deadline upon them, and no time to check the story, the journalists wrote a rather flippant account of J. Numa Damiens' visit for that week's edition, and concluded it with this folksy appeal to their readers: 'Please, Sister and Brother, won't you come to our rescue and tell us what's ailing folks who say fish are raining from heaven on a clear sunshiny day!'

It turned out that the paper had been wrong to scoff. By the time it hit the newsstands, eyewitnesses to the fish-fall had come forward with their own amazing tales to tell. Thirty years later, many of them could vividly recall what happened.

Said Anthony Roy Jnr: 'As I left the house to go to school that morning, I went through the back of the house, and as I got near the garage I heard something fall on the tin roof of the garage and simultaneously something hit me on my head and on my shoulders, and when I looked down I saw they were fish.'

Mrs Eddie Gremillion was ill at the time: 'I was in bed, not feeling good, and I didn't get up early. But my maid came early and she was out in the yard. She ran in excited like anything, and she's a black maid but that day she was white with excitement, and she came and she told me, "Miss Lola, Miss Lola," she said, "it's raining fishes. It's raining fishes."'

Mrs Elmire Roy's maid also panicked: 'When the fish fell on the tin roof, my maid, whose name was Viola, ran outside with me, and she was so upset, and she kept saying, "Lord, Lord, it must be the end of the world."'

Sheriff 'Potch' Didier was another witness. He was driving through Marksville at the time. 'I saw the fish fall out of the sky,' he said. 'I kept driving. I was very amazed.'

At one house, the yard was 'just absolutely covered with fish. And just about that time some other people started getting here and everybody was just amazed at the whole thing, and we just couldn't believe it, believe that the fish had just dropped out of the sky.'

Yet the Marksville fish-fall, astonishing as it was to the citizens of the town, is not unique. All kinds of weird showers have been reported over the centuries, notably of fish, blocks of ice, and frogs. We marvelled at many such mysteries in *Arthur C. Clarke's Mysterious World*, but could offer little in the way of satisfactory explanation. However, recent work by researchers studying fresh cases and re-evaluating many from the past has provided a new understanding of how it is that fish and frogs can rain from the sky.

In the past, many experts flatly rejected the claims of eyewitnesses. For example, in 1859 a sawyer called John Lewis from the Aberdare Valley in Wales told this story to the local vicar, the Reverend John Griffith:

On Wednesday, February 9, I was getting out a piece of timber, for the purpose of setting it for the saw, when I was startled by something falling all over me – down my neck, on my head, and on my back. On putting my hand down my neck I was surprised to find they were little fish. By this time I saw the whole ground covered with them. I took off my hat, the brim of which was full of them. They were jumping all about.

Lewis added that the fish had arrived in two showers, about ten minutes apart. He and his workmates gathered some of them up and sent a few to London Zoo, where they were put on display. Although they proved a popular attraction, not everyone was impressed. J. E. Gray of the British Museum told the *Zoological Magazine*: 'On reading the evidence it appears to me most probably to be only a practical joke of the mates of John Lewis, who seem to have thrown a pailful of water with the fish in it over him.' Edward Newman agreed: 'Dr Gray is without doubt correct in attributing the whole affair to some practical joker.'

There are certainly reasons to be wary of frog-falls. Just because the creatures suddenly appear in large numbers at the same time as a shower, it does not mean that they have actually come down with the rain. In many cases the rain has simply brought the frogs out from their usual hiding places to enjoy the water. Early in this century, one observer put it rather quaintly:

The little creatures have doffed their tadpole tails and have wandered in their thousands far afield. During the day a crack in the ground, a dead leaf, or an empty snail shell affords them shelter, and during the night they travel in pursuit of small insects. Then comes the shower of rain. It fills the cracks in the ground, washes away the dead leaves, and chokes up the snail shell with mud-splashes. But what matter? The little frogs are all over the place, revelling in the longed-for moisture ...

During a torrential downpour in August 1986, Melvin Harris of Hadleigh, Essex, happened to be out walking in the streets near his home. Shortly after the rain started he noticed a few frogs and toads, an uncommon sight in the suburbs. Soon there were dozens of them hopping about. He is certain that none came from the sky, and indeed watched several actually creeping out of nooks and crannies.

Sudden frog migrations have also caused confusion. When thousands of the hopping creatures appeared in Towyn, North Wales, in 1947, many of the townspeople believed that they had fallen from the sky. Three days after the invasion had begun, desperate

householders were still trying to clear them
from their property. 'They're swarming like
bees,' said one weary citizen. It turns out that
frog migrations are common around Towyn,
for the town is situated between two
marshes. One eyewitness, Jack Roberts,
pointed out that 1947 was a vintage year for
frogs. There were plenty of tadpoles in the
spring and the summer was extremely wet.

Writer Francis Hitching discovered that a
plague of frogs at Chalon-sur-Saône in
France in 1922 was also almost certainly
simply a mass-migration, although Charles
Fort, the great collector of these and similar

tales, had decided that they must have fallen
from the sky. In 1979 Hitching checked the
story while passing through the French town
and concluded, '. . . it seems clear that what
had happened was a migratory plague of
frogs crossing the roads. Observers remembered being unable to avoid squashing them
as they bicycled. No one had seen them dropping from the sky.'

In this century a few apparent 'rains' of
fish were caused, as it turned out, by birds
dropping their prey in flight. For example,
in Australia at Forbes, New South Wales,
fish – some of them weighing up to ½ lb –

Joe Alpin with his wife Dorrien. One evening during the Second World War the sky darkened and 'millions' of frogs rained down on him.

fell from the mouths of hundreds of passing pelicans on to astonished observers below, and in 1979 a golfer was struck on the head by an airborne red mullet dropped by a clumsy gull.

Yet such explanations do not account for every case. Many reliable eyewitnesses have actually described seeing fish and frogs fall when there has not been a bird in sight, let alone the large flock necessary to convey the shoals of airborne creatures that have landed on or around them.

In 1948 Mr Ian Patey, a former British Amateur Golf Champion, was playing a round on a course at Barton-on-Sea, near Bournemouth. His wife was about to play a shot. But,

> just before she hit it, a fish fell down on the ground in front of us. And then we looked up

in the sky and suddenly there were hundreds of fish falling in an area of about a hundred yards. They were live, they were larger than whitebait, possibly smaller than a sardine. My reaction was one of complete surprise. After all, there wasn't a cloud in the sky.

During the Second World War, Joe Alpin was stationed with the Artists' Rifles at an English stately home, Alton Towers in Staffordshire. One evening he was driving through the deer park in an army truck:

> The sky suddenly darkened – very very dark indeed, like a thunderstorm. And then the frogs came, millions of them, raining out of the sky, millions upon millions of frogs about half an inch long. They fell all over us, all over the grass, all over the cars, down the neck of our tunics, on our feet, hands, everywhere. It rained frogs for at least an hour and a quarter.

At Esh Winning in County Durham in 1887 Mr Edward Cook, realizing that a storm was approaching, took shelter with his horse and rolley cart beneath the gables of a house.

In a few minutes large drops of rain began to fall, and with them, to my astonishment, scores of small frogs (about the size of a man's thumbnail) jumping about in all directions; and, as there was no dam or grass near, I could not imagine wherever they came from, until the storm was over and I had mounted the waggon again. Then I found several of the little gentlemen on the rolley, and knew they must have come down with the rain, it being impossible for them to have leaped so high.

In 1960 Grace Wright reported a similar experience to a magazine:

More than 50 years ago, I was walking along a street in Hounslow with my husband and small son when a heavy storm broke. We first thought they were hailstones until we saw they were all tiny frogs and were jumping about. My son filled a sweet-box to take home. The brim of my husband's hat was full of frogs while the storm lasted. They were everywhere.

On 28 August 1977 thousands of tiny frogs – some apparently no larger than peas – poured down on to Canet-Plage near Perpignan, France. Eyewitnesses said they bounced off the bonnets of cars.

In October 1986, *The Journal of Meteorology* published this vivid eyewitness account. It came from J. W. Roberts of Kettering, Northamptonshire, who, in 1919, was working at a farm during the school holidays.

I was walking between the stacks of hay and straw when there was a sudden rush of air. I looked up towards a disused quarry cutting and I saw a dark, almost black, cloud coming rushing towards me. It was a whirlwind. It picked up some of the loose straw lying about, and when it reached the buildings it seemed to stop, and the dark cloud suddenly fell down and

I was smothered all over with small frogs – thousands of them about 1¼ to 1½ inches long. I think they must have come from a lake a mile away up the cutting. Oh boy, was I scared. I ran across the footbridge over the brook right close to our house, and my mother could hardly believe me, only I had small frogs in my shirt, etc.

From earliest times, the theory usually advanced to explain these weird falls has been that the frogs and fish are carried aloft by freak winds, tornadoes or waterspouts. The creatures fall back to earth when the wind weakens. Tornadoes and whirlwinds certainly do play extraordinary tricks. For example, when a tornado passed through the Brahmaputra district of India in March 1875, a dead cow was found up in the branches of a tree, about 30 ft from the ground. After a tornado had hit Oklahoma in 1905, the Associated Press reported that 'all the corpses in the track of the storm were found without shoes'; at Lansing, Michigan, in 1943, thirty chickens were found sitting in a row stripped entirely of their feathers; and on 30 May 1951 people clearing up after a tornado at Scottsbluff, Nebraska, found that a bean had been driven deep into an egg without cracking the shell. At St Louis in 1896 a whirlwind was reported to have lifted a carriage into the air. It was apparently then carried along for 100 yards before being allowed to float back to earth so gently that the coachman's hat remained firmly on his head! In *Tornadoes of the United States*, Snowden D. Flora tells the remarkable tale of two Texans, known only as Al and Bill, who chanced to be at Al's home in Higgins, Texas, on 9 April 1947 when a tornado struck.

Al, hearing the roar, stepped to the door and opened it to see what was happening. It was

Waterspouts, like this one photographed near Hurst Castle, Hampshire, may be responsible for some fish and frog falls. The creatures are carried aloft and fall back to earth when the spout weakens.

torn from his grasp and disappeared. He was carried away, over the tree tops. Bill went to the door to investigate the disappearance of his friend and found himself, also, sailing through the Texas atmosphere, but in a slightly different direction from the course his friend was taking. Both landed about two hundred feet from the house with only minor injuries. Al started back and found Bill uncomfortably wrapped in wire. He unwound his friend and both headed for Al's house, crawling because the wind was too strong to walk against. They reached the site of the house only to find that all the house except the floor had disappeared. The almost incredible part of the story is that Al's wife and two children were huddled on a divan, uninjured. The only other piece of furniture left on the floor was a lamp.

If the wind can lift two beefy Texans and an Indian cow into the air, fish and frogs must present no problem, and many fish- and frog-falls do turn out, on close investigation, to occur at times when unusual winds are recorded. This is certainly true in the case of the Marksville fish-fall. We know this because, by a remarkable coincidence, one of the first people to reach the fish-strewn streets of the town was a biologist working for the US Department of Wild Life and Fisheries. A. D. Bajkov and his wife had been having breakfast in a restaurant when a bemused waitress told them that fish were raining down outside. The Bajkovs rushed to the sidewalk, their food forgotten, and at once set about identifying the airborne shoal.

'They were freshwater fish native to local waters', Bajkov later reported in a letter to the American journal, *Science*. He found large-mouth black bass, goggle-eyes, two species of sunfish, hickory shad, and several kinds of minnows. There were more shad than anything else. Bajkov collected a jar-full of prize specimens for distribution to

museums. Like a good scientist, he also took careful note of the weather conditions.

> The actual falling of the fish occurred in somewhat short intervals, during foggy and comparatively calm weather. The velocity of the wind on the ground did not exceed eight miles per hour. The New Orleans weather bureau had no report of any large tornado, or updrift, in the vicinity of Marksville at that time. However, James Nelson Gowanloch, chief biologist for the Louisiana Department of Wild Life and Fisheries, and I had noticed the presence of numerous small tornadoes, or 'devil dusters' the day before the 'rain of fish' in Marksville.

A more obvious connection between a fall and unusual weather conditions was noted in a letter sent to the *East Anglian Magazine* in 1958. The writer, H. Bye, had overheard a conversation between an old farmhand and a group of workers. The farmhand was telling them 'that at West Row and Isleham, on the Cambridge/Suffolk border, when he was a young man, a waterspout was seen over the River Lark. Some hours afterwards there was a heavy thunderstorm and it rained frogs.'

A waterspout also blew up near the site of another English frog-fall in 1892, according to *Symons's Monthly Meteorological Magazine*:

> During the storm that raged with considerable fury in Birmingham on Wednesday morning, June 30, a shower of frogs fell in the suburb of Moseley. They were found scattered about several gardens. Almost white in colour, they had evidently been absorbed in a small waterspout that was driven over Birmingham by the tempest.

In 1982 Michael W. Rowe, writing in the *Journal of Meteorology*, revealed that he had discovered a graphic account of fish cascading from a waterspout. It occurs in a book

called *The Excitement*, published in 1830. According to the story, some travellers were sailing through the Strait of Malacca in about 1760, when:

> They were surrounded with waterspouts, one of which was very near, and they fired to disperse it. The roaring was tremendous, and presently a torrent of water poured on the ship, which brought down with it many fish and weeds; yet the water was perfectly fresh; a phenomenon singularly curious.

Fish have actually been seen inside or emerging from waterspouts and whirlwinds. E. W. Gudger of the American Museum of Natural History, an avid collector of reports of mysterious showers, was told by his friend, E. A. McIlhenny of Avery Island, Louisiana, of 'a small waterspout on a fresh-water distributary in the Mississippi delta, which broke just in front of his fishing boats and then filled boats with water and fishes'.

Michael Rowe also dug out this tiny paragraph from *The Times* of 23 January 1936: 'Violent whirlwinds accompanied a storm which broke over Florence on Monday, and among various objects which were seen spinning in the air were some big fish which had evidently been drawn from the River Arno.' Rowe collects reports of whirlwinds and often writes to local papers appealing for information. A letter in the *Manchester Evening News* brought this response from E. Singleton, who reported seeing fish and frogs actually 'taking off' at Newton-le-Willows, Lancashire, in 1947:

> I saw flocks of birds suddenly appear from behind me. Looking back, the reason was obvious, for approaching rapidly was a whirlwind which was carrying all sorts of debris. I threw my two children to the floor and lay on top of them while the wind passed by about 30 yards away. It travelled directly over a huge pond which

was locally known as Thompson's Pit. Half the water together with fish, frogs and weed was carried away and was found deposited on house tops half-a-mile away.

Sometimes, ponds, lakes and rivers are completely emptied of water by the wind. Snowden D. Flora, in *Tornadoes of the United States*, notes an example: 'When the destructive tornado of June 23, 1944, passed over West Fork River, West Virginia, the water was actually sucked up and the river left dry, momentarily, at the place where the storm crossed it.'

Another collector of meteorological curiosities, Waldo L. McAtee of the US Biological Survey, told the Biological Society of Washington of two similar 'lift-offs'. The first was at Christiansoe on the island of Bornholm, Denmark, where 'a waterspout emptied the harbor to such an extent that the greater part of the bottom was uncovered'. The other took place at a town in France. There had been a violent storm overnight: 'When morning dawned, the streets were found strewed with fish of various sizes. The mystery was soon solved, for a fish pond in the vicinity had been blown dry and only the large fish left behind.'

Yet even though freak winds are almost certainly the cause of these exotic rains of fish and frogs, the scientists have not yet found all the answers. For example, who could have blamed Major J. Hedgepath, US Army (retired), for being totally baffled by a discovery he made while stationed on the island of Guam in September 1936? He told the readers of *Science*: 'I witnessed a brief rainfall of fish, one of the specimens of which was identified as the tench (*Tinca tinca*) which, to my knowledge, is common only to the fresh waters of Europe. The presence of this species at a locale so remote from its normal habitat is worthy of note.'

Indeed it is. Guam is the largest of the Mariana Islands. It lies in the Western Pacific.

The Jelly Meteors

What is gelatinous, smelly and said to fall from shooting stars? The answer is *Pwdre Ser* (Welsh for 'star rot'), a strange jelly-like substance which, eyewitnesses have reported, rains down from the sky.

In 1978 Mrs M. Ephgrave of Cambridge told a television weatherman about a mysterious substance which had landed on her lawn during a heavy rainstorm: 'It glided down, [it was] about the size of a football and settled like a jelly.' Other reports from earlier times describe a 'round patch as broad as a bushel, which looked thick, slimy and black' seen on Dartmoor in 1638; a 'gelatinous mass of a greyish colour so viscid as to "tremble all over" when poked with a stick' that hit Koblenz in 1844; and a 'body of fetid jelly, 4 feet in diameter' found by villagers from Loweville, New York, in 1846.

So what is *Pwdre Ser*? Sadly, not 'star slime', the last vestige of a shooting star, despite Sir Walter Scott's assertion, 'Seek a fallen star and thou shalt only light on some foul jelly.' There are probably several more mundane explanations. Some examples – if the jelly was not actually seen falling – may be colonies of blue-green algae, known as *Nostoc commune*, a fungus called *Tremella mesenterica*, or even leftovers from the innards of frogs and toads devoured by birds.

Few samples have been analysed by scientists. The Cambridge jelly, for example, apparently disappeared overnight, but more than two centuries earlier, in 1712, the Reverend John Morton of Emmanuel College, Cambridge, boiled some *Pwdre Ser* and found it contained fragments of animal bones and skin. He also added two valuable observations: that he had seen a wounded gull vomit a jelly-like substance which turned out to be a ball of half-digested earthworms; and that a friend, Sir William Craven, had watched a bittern do the same thing.

In 1980 Dr G. T. Meaden, Editor of the *Journal of Meteorology*, seized a rare opportunity and sent a small sample from a blob of colourless jelly found in the garden of Mr Philip Buller at Hemel Hempstead, Hertfordshire, for analysis. The scientist, Mr T. J. Turvey, had only about 1 dessertspoon (10 ml) of the stuff to work on, but he was still able to isolate all kinds of material in it, including plant debris, freshwater algae, roundworms and bacteria. His conclusion: that it was material which a creature normally found near fresh water, such as a heron, might first have swallowed and then regurgitated.

These, then, are clues which point to a solution to the *Pwdre Ser* mystery. Yet the full answer must wait for the day when a scientist can both observe and catch a falling 'star slime'.

Arthur C. Clarke writes on 'Icebergs of Space'

One of the subjects we investigated in some detail in *Arthur C. Clarke's Mysterious World* (Chapter 2: A Cabinet of Curiosities) was that of objects falling from the sky. This has been happening for centuries before the coming of the Air Age, and has involved an amazing range of materials – as well as living creatures, such as frogs and fish. In some cases there can be little doubt of the explanation. On the theory 'What comes down must go up' we asked for eyewitness reports of such 'lift-offs' and, as you have seen, were happy to receive some.

The hailstones that fell on Girard, Illinois, in 1929 were
bigger than hens' eggs, but even larger 'aerial icebergs'
have been recorded, including one 20 ft (6 m) in
diameter.

The most spectacular and perhaps well-attested of all falls, however, consist of *ice*, sometimes in masses far too large to be explained as abnormal hail formations. This is a genuine mystery – but now, at last, we have an answer, though it may not be the only one. It involves a distinguished visitor whom I am sure you will all remember. If you don't see the connection at first, please be patient . . .

The week before Christmas, 1985, I made my first serious attempt to locate Halley's Comet. According to the Ephemeris in *The Handbook of the British Astronomical Association*, it would be almost directly above Colombo soon after sunset; unfortunately, a rather misty sky was suffused with light from the waxing moon, so I had no great expectation of success. Another observational hazard was the glare of floodlights from the garden of my next-door neighbour, the Iraqi Ambassador. (His concern for security was understandable: a few days later the papers reported a shootout at his front gate with the local Iranians.)

I fitted my 8-in Celestron with the lowest-power eyepiece available ($\times$ 50 – even lower would have been better to look for a faint but fairly large object) and set it up on the flat roof, lining up the polar axis by the tiles, whose orientation I'd determined years ago. Such a crude procedure was hardly good enough for astrophotography, but quite adequate for visual observations. When the clock drive is switched on, an object will stay in view for an hour or more before drifting out of the field.

Now I had to aim the telescope at the exact point in the depressingly luminous sky. Luckily, there were some convenient signposts available – the brilliant planet Jupiter,

and the stars in Aquarius, particularly the brightest one, Alpha, which is almost exactly on the Equator. By a stroke of luck, so was the comet on the night of 20 December, so once I'd found Alpha Aquarius only a very slight north–south correction should be necessary.

The conditions were such that I couldn't locate the third magnitude star Alpha visually. No problem; first I got Jupiter in the centre of the field, and adjusted the telescope's right ascension and declination (the celestial equivalents of longitude and latitude) circles so that they agreed with the planet's tabulated position in *The BAA Handbook*. Then I moved east and north along the two circles to RA 22 hours 05 minutes plus ½ degree – and there was Alpha in the low-powered finder telescope. It was nowhere near the middle of the field (after all, I'd only aligned the polar axis by eye) so I made another slight adjustment to compensate for the remaining error. Now I was sure that I was in reasonable agreement with the celestial coordinate system, and was ready for the final step.

Very carefully, I slewed the telescope through the calculated arc – about 10 degrees eastwards and a smidgen north. Then, holding my breath and covering my head with a black cloth like an old-time photographer, I peered into the eyepiece.

I didn't really expect to see anything. Quite apart from the poor seeing conditions, my field of vision was only ½ degree across – about the size of the moon, which is much smaller than most people realize. (Try covering it with your thumbnail some night.) It was more than likely that the residual errors of adjustment had caused me to miss my target, which meant that I'd have to do some searching.

Arthur C. Clarke viewed Halley's Comet through his
8-in telescope from the roof of his house in Colombo, Sri
Lanka.

I could hardly believe my luck – there it was, shyly but unmistakably lurking at the edge of the field! A slight twist of the declination screw, and it was properly centred. Honesty compels me to admit that it was not a conspicuous object; just a bit fainter, and it wouldn't have been visible at all. But it was *there*, and that was the only thing that mattered.

My first glimpse of the most famous of comets, still heading for its once-in-a-human-lifetime appointment with the sun, has left an indelible photographic image in my memory. It appeared as a misty blob of light, a few times the size of the planet Jupiter as I'd seen it with the same magnification just minutes earlier. Although it grew brighter towards the centre, there was no nucleus – no star-like condensation of light at its core, as is shown by many comets. Nor was I able to see any trace of a tail, though that was not surprising. Halley was still a long way from the sun, and its witch's cauldron of volatile ices and organic chemicals had not yet come to the boil.

As I watched that ghostly apparition glimmering in the field of my telescope, I could not help thinking that a small fleet of spacecraft was on its way to meet the comet in less than three months' time. How amazed – and excited – Halley would have been by this rendezvous with the visitor that will always bear his name! And perhaps *Giotto,* the *Vegas* and the *Planets,* when their mountains of data were analysed – a process which could take years – would confirm that comets are indeed responsible for those massive ice-falls from a cloudless sky which have intrigued man for centuries.

Today, of course, many such events can be all too easily explained: lumps of ice up to 12 lb (5.5 kilos) in weight can accumulate on high-flying aircraft until shaken or blown off. Chemical analysis has sometimes revealed their origin; if, as in one report, there are 'traces of coffee, tea and detergent', there's no need to invoke comets (though perhaps that doesn't exclude UFOs). But we must look for another explanation in the case of the 20-ft (6-m)-diameter block that fell on an estate in Scotland. Maybe a Jumbo jet with serious plumbing problems could produce such a mini-iceberg; however, Boeing 747s were not very common at the time of the report – 1849. Comets, on the other hand, have been around longer than the earth itself; they are part of the debris left over from the construction of the solar system.

It has long been suspected that many, if not most comets consist largely of ice – or, to be more accurate, of *ices*. In ordinary life, the only variety we encounter is frozen water, but in the extremely cold regions far from the sun where comets spend most of their lives it comes in many other flavours. There's ammonia ice, methane ice, carbon dioxide ice (well-known in the refrigeration industry under the name 'dry ice') and still more exotic varieties. As a comet heads sunwards, most of these vaporize beyond the orbit of the earth; but frozen water can survive not only the increasing radiation but even – if the initial mass is large enough – the frictional heat caused by passage through the atmosphere.

It seems very likely that some ice-falls are of cosmic origin: they are associated with the sonic booms heard when vehicles re-enter the earth's atmosphere. It's a strange thought that the largest of all icebergs do not lie off the coast of Antarctica, but drift between the stars.

And at least once during this century, in 1908, one may have crashed upon this planet.

Halley's Comet – a 'witch's cauldron of volatile ices and organic chemicals' – photographed from Alice Springs, Australia, on 8 April 1986.

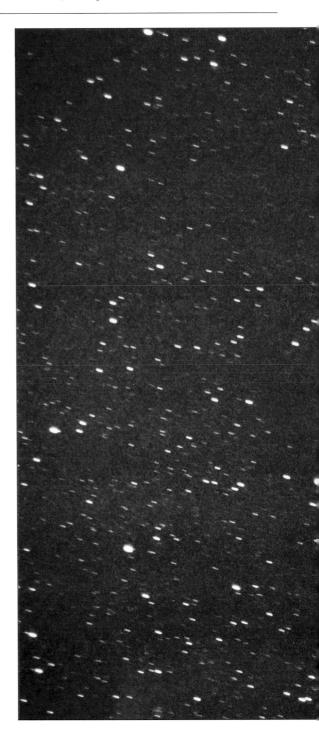

The famous Tunguska 'event' (see page 73) has long been a mystery because no substantial meteoric debris was ever found. But a mass of ice moving at fifty times the speed of a rifle bullet could do megatons worth of damage, and leave no evidence of the crime. (I recall a murder story in which there was no weapon; it turned out to have been a dagger made of ice. As Einstein remarked, 'Nature too can be subtle.')

The idea that there is a lot of ice floating round in space has a disreputable pseudo-scientific ancestry – which may be why astronomers have been slow to accept it. The American collector of enigmas and anomalies, Charles Fort, suggested that there may be 'vast fields of aerial ice from which pieces occasionally break away'. Except for the word 'aerial' this may indeed be almost true.

These speculations on Halley's Comet have triggered a memory of more than fifty years ago. My very first attempt at a full-length science-fiction story (fortunately long since destroyed) concerned that typical disaster of the spaceways, the collision between an interplanetary liner and a large meteorite – or small comet, if you prefer. I was quite proud of the title: *Icebergs of Space* – never dreaming at the time that such things really existed. I have always been a little too fond of surprise endings. In the last line I revealed the name of the wrecked spaceship. It was SS – wait for it – *Titanic*.

Don't laugh. Sooner or later, it will happen again.

The above note was composed, believe it or not, on Christmas Day 1985; for as long as I can remember I have escaped to my office as soon as the compulsory festivities are over. Since then, there have been a few more developments.

Halley's Comet, to the surprise of everyone except Sir Fred Hoyle and Dr Chandra Wickramesinghe (who used the observations to support their controversial theory that comets may harbour bacteria and other life-forms), turned out to be very black indeed. It was not, as expected, a 'dirty snowball' – but a 'snowy dirtball'. However, it certainly did contain vast quantities of ice, and my thesis still stands. It has now received support from several unexpected directions. On 13 August 1984 a report came from Moscow headlined, FROZEN GAS METEORITE HITS RUSSIAN HOLIDAY CAMP; part of it reads:

> A Russian holiday camp supervisor who narrowly missed being struck by a block of ice falling from a cloudless sky has provided Soviet scientists with their first sample of an 'ice meteorite'. Anatoly Kozhukhov heard a whizzing noise and jumped out of the path of the chunk of ice which thudded into the sand two paces away from him at a holiday camp near Kazan on the River Volga. He put the strange object in his refrigerator and called Moscow scientists, who sent a team of researchers. Their conclusion was that the camp had been struck by the remnants of frozen gas meteorites which had penetrated the atmosphere. Ice meteorites had landed on earth before but melted before scientists could analyze their chemical composition, Tass said.

Thank you, Tass; just what I've been saying. But the final remark isn't quite correct. In our *Mysterious World* programme scientists in England and the USA actually analyzed ice-falls that had been saved. And the Chinese had got hold of a sample a year earlier than the Russian one, for on 11 April 1983 a 100 lb (40 kilo) 'cake' of ice dropped out of the sky and splintered on the pavement in the East China city of Wuxi. By an ingenious piece of detective work the Chinese scientists were able to make its meteoric origin virtually certain. On a picture taken seventeen minutes later by the US metsat *NOAA-7*, they discovered a dark line running across the clouds towards the impact point! They believe it was the track made by the meteor (original mass probably about a ton) as it entered the atmosphere.

Artificial satellites may also have contributed another clue to this continuing story. Astrophysicist Louis Frank of the University of Iowa has discovered that ultra-violet images of the upper atmosphere made by *Dynamics Explorer 1* show numerous black spots, lasting a few minutes which he believes are produced by water vapour from incoming 'ice comets'. If this is confirmed it may throw new light on both planetary and biological evolution. The ice comets – if that's what they are – arrive at a rate of over 1,000 an hour, and average 100 tons each. If this has been going on for the whole of geological time, it's enough to account for all the oceans of the earth! This will upset a lot of theories; no wonder that a good deal of arm-waving is going on among Dr Frank's sceptical colleagues.

Perhaps they feel that all this is uncomfortably reminiscent of the 'cosmic ice' theories put forward early in this century by eccentric Germans like Fauth and Hoerbiger, who believed that most of the universe was made of ice and that, for example, lunar formations were carved by glaciers. (Though I wouldn't swear to it, I seem to recall that one genius constructed a cosmology in which even the *sun* was made of ice!) Such pseudo-science flourished – briefly – under the Nazis; how ironic if it turns out, after all, to contain an element of truth.

The Tunguska site in the Eastern Soviet Union and the extent of the devastation.

Overleaf: Lake Nios, Cameroon, where 1,700 people and countless animals died as a result of breathing poisoned gas.

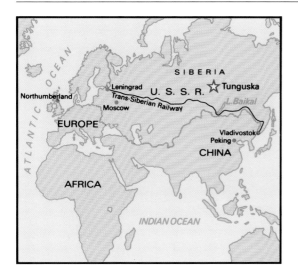

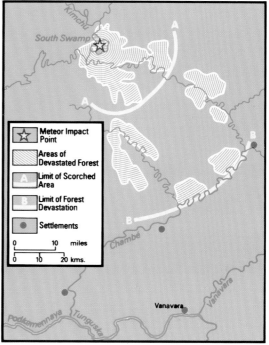

Further Thoughts on Tunguska

The weight of scientific opinion now favours the idea that it was a comet which exploded above Siberia in 1908, laying waste to around 800 square miles of forest. Indeed, in the summer of 1986 the American Geophysical Union held a special session in Baltimore, Maryland, designed to alert the world, in that year of Halley's return, to the catastrophic implications of another comet arriving and colliding with the earth.

The geophysicists have a special nightmare. Rocks and boulders – the debris of space – are swirling round the earth all the time, running into our atmosphere and disintegrating. On average, a 1,000-ton boulder bumps into us each month. Frequently, especially in June, there are spectacular displays of shooting stars at night as fragments burn up in the upper atmosphere. But what the geophysicists fear is the arrival of a really large body weighing perhaps 100,000 tons or more. They envisage its sudden appearance, unanticipated, in the upper atmosphere. There would be a tremendous fireball,

brighter than the sun; then a cataclysmic explosion. If this took place over a populated area, the destruction and loss of life would be enormous. Worse, it might well be assumed that the explosion was a thermonuclear weapon, with the consequent horror of retaliation and holocaust. Hopefully the sensor systems of the superpowers are, or soon will be, discriminating enough to tell the difference.

However, in September 1986 another natural disaster occurred which, some scientists felt, might shed light on the mystery of Tunguska. In Yaounde, capital of the West African state of Cameroon, the authorities started to receive reports that in an area around Lake Nios in the interior, hundreds of people had just fallen down dead. Officials who quickly arrived on the scene were confronted with an apocalyptic vision. The roll-

Below: Carcasses of cattle lie where the gas overtook them around Lake Nios.

ing green countryside was strewn with the carcasses of cattle, pigs and wild animals. Along the roads and tracks leading to the lake lay the corpses of people who had apparently been struck down as they walked or bicycled along. In the villages themselves around the lake, people had died by the hundred in their houses and gardens. In total, more than 1,700 people died, as well as herds of animals. It was soon apparent that a great cloud of poisonous gas was responsible. It had rolled down from the crater lake, fatally enveloping everything in its path.

In 1984 a geologist, A. R. Crawford of the University of Canterbury, New Zealand, suggested that a great gas cloud from within the earth might have been the cause of the Tunguska explosion. Tunguska, he wrote,

'might be a wholly terrestrial phenomenon . . . Rather than being the only well-argued-for cometary impact on Earth, it may be the only modern example of a sudden very voluminous hot gaseous effusion.' Crawford noted that such gases were associated with diamond-bearing kimberlite pipes, a belt of which lie across Siberia.

Crawford belongs to a school of geologists which believes that the earth may be expanding, even pulsating like a heart, and that this may account for some of the fractures associated with plate tectonics. From these fractures in the earth's crust may emerge gouts of lethal and explosive gases.

Sixty years of research on the Tunguska site have still failed to come up with any convincing residue of extra-terrestrial ma-

terial, though there are plenty of exotic minerals in the little glass globules found in the Tunguska soil. It is a frightening but plausible concept that the big bang, which could have laid waste a city the size of Paris, might simply have been the biggest gas explosion the modern world has ever seen.

Arthur C. Clarke comments

The Tunguska event will soon be eighty years in the past. Imagine our surprise, therefore, at receiving this report in 1985 from Mr Samuel Sunter of Victoria, Canada. Mr Sunter was a boy of nine, living in Northumberland, England, when the explosion took place. This is what he told us:

> I saw, looking north east, on June 30th 1908, a large red ball of fire, about three times the size of a full moon. It looked just like a hole in the sky. On the other side of the hole, it looked like flames, just like looking into the fire box of a locomotive. But what made me afraid was a solid beam of light which reached right down to where I was standing. This made me afraid and I ran into the house, so I do not know how long it lasted after I first saw it. Even today I have a very vivid memory of it.

Could Mr Sunter have indeed seen the Tunguska explosion from 4,000 miles away across the roof of the world? It seems improbable; but if his memory of the date is correct, he almost certainly witnessed some of its effects.

The whole subject of meteor – or cometary – impact has now become of great scientific and, surprisingly, *political* importance. On the scientific side, it is now widely believed that the extinction of the dinosaurs (as well as a vast range of other creatures) some sixty-five million years ago was due to the impact of an asteroid or comet about 5 miles in diameter. Quite apart from the colossal

immediate damage, the resulting smoke and airborne debris darkened the earth for months, killing off much of the planet's vegetation and the chains of life that were based upon it.

Nobel Prize winning physicist Luis Alvarez, who with his son Walter is chiefly responsible for this explanation of the 'Cretaceous-Tertiary extinction', has no doubts about its truth. Twenty-five years ago I dedicated my only *non*-science-fiction novel, *Glide-Path*, to Luis and his wartime radiation lab colleagues, with whom I worked in 1942. When I recently updated the Preface, I mentioned that the debate over his theory 'now rages furiously'. He corrected me at once:

> had you written that sentence a few years ago, I couldn't disagree. But now, the ball game is over, and *everyone* who has taken the trouble to examine the evidence is convinced that we were right ... Our theory – more accurately our *discovery* – that the K-T extinction was caused by the impact of a 10-kilometre diameter object is no longer controversial, in the scientific sense of that word.

Certainly controversial, however, is the theory that even a small-scale exchange of nuclear weapons could cause similar ecological effects, so that the whole world, and not merely the target areas, would be devastated by the effects of a 'nuclear winter'. If this is true, the entire human race is held hostage by the stockpiles of a few nations.

Perhaps evolution is about to repeat itself. It may well be that we mammals would still be scurrying nervously in the undergrowth if a multi-megaton explosion sixty-five million years ago had not eliminated the giant beasts who were then the masters of the earth. Are we about to repeat the scenario – and make way for *our* successors – the cockroaches?

Janet & Colin

Proboscis

Eyes

Inner Arms (6)

Outer

Funnel

Probable form
Elephant Squid
Cephalopod Ness

Is the Loch Ness monster a giant squid? Anthony Shiels, who advanced this theory in 1984, drew this impression of what Nessie may really look like.

Below: Sharon Boulton and Catriona Murray indicate the spot near Urquhart Castle, Loch Ness, where they claim they saw a huge dark shape emerge repeatedly from the water.

4.

Strange Tales from the Lakes

The waves came crashing into the shore and we both immediately rushed to see what was happening. Only minutes before we had remarked on the stillness of the loch.

There was obviously something very large in the water moving at great speed close to the shore.

Initially, I could see one black hump-like object but it submerged. Then within seconds I could see two objects, one of which I took to be the tail.

I watched spellbound for some time before the creature dived deeply, creating a considerable displacement of water and disappeared.

Thus Mrs Dilys Fisher, a teacher from the south of England, claimed to have spotted the Loch Ness monster in August 1982. At the time of the sighting, Mrs Fisher and her husband were repairing a hired moped in a lay-by on the A82 Inverness to Fort William road. As they tinkered with the engine, they heard 'a sudden, violent movement' in the loch.

Four years later, in August 1986, three teenaged girls working for the summer at the Loch Ness Hotel, Drumnadrochit, were standing near Urquhart Castle, a picturesque ruin on the northern shore. It was near midnight. The loch was quiet. But they claim that when they looked out over the water, they saw a dark shape in the middle of the loch.

'It had a large hump at one end and a smaller hump at the other,' said Catriona Murray. 'At first we thought it was an island,

but then we realized there are no islands in that part of Loch Ness.'

Catriona's companion, Sharon Boulton, was equally astonished. 'It kept appearing and disappearing,' she said, 'and, despite its massive size, we could not hear a sound. It could not have been an illusion because we all saw it.'

The girls tried to rouse the occupants of a nearby house, but no one stirred. Instead, they stopped a passing milk lorry and its driver obligingly shone his headlights over the water. But there was nothing unusual to be seen: just the glinting water, unruffled by humps.

As these stories suggest, public interest in

The Goodyear blimp *Europa* surveys the Loch in 1982.
The Loch Ness Project research barge can be seen on
the water near Urquhart Castle.

the puzzle of the Loch Ness monster has not declined in recent years. The dedicated hunters have been as active as ever, and so, apparently, has Nessie herself, for eye-witnesses continue to come forward with claimed sightings of the world's most famous lake monster. Most ambitious of all the recent schemes to find definitive proof of Nessie's existence came in 1984, when a huge tubular trap, 80 ft (25 m) long and made of fibreglass, was airlifted into the loch. Despite rising winds, helicopter pilot Jim Wood dropped it precisely on target off Horseshoe Scree near Fort Augustus; and the trap's designer, a twenty-five-year-old civil servant called Steve Whittle, his sponsors – a vodka company – and the British public, settled down to the kind of wait every fisherman knows is essential to ensure a catch.

> Whatever she is, [said Whittle] Nessie must be aware of exactly what is going on in the loch, every corner of which she will know as well as you or I know our own living rooms.
>
> For that reason, we have made the trap as flimsy in appearance as possible, and will leave her to get used to it for a couple of weeks. She will undoubtedly be afraid of it at first, but will eventually see salmon and trout swimming through it as they become accustomed to its presence.
>
> Then, hopefully, she will become braver and will not be able to resist the temptation of a concentration of a shoal of 40 salmon in one place.

But patience was not rewarded. The trap – designed merely to detain the monster for photography and examination by a zoologist – was never sprung.

Other researchers took to the air in the Goodyear blimp *Europa*, but its crew of twenty-five failed to spot anything out of the ordinary as they cruised above the loch at a stately thirty-five miles per hour.

Monster-hunter Steve Whittle watches as his 'Nessie trap' is lowered by helicopter into Loch Ness in August 1984.

Theories advanced to explain the monster's elusive nature and its reasons for taking up residence in Loch Ness have become weirder and wilder. 'Is Nessie a Giant Squid?' asked a writer in Britain's journal of strange phenomena, *Fortean Times*. Meanwhile, in 1983, monster-hunter Eric Beckjord explained his new idea to reporters:

> I am beginning to think of it this way: you need a pair of polaroid glasses to see the laminations on your car windscreen.
>
> What if there is a monster and it has quasi- or pseudo-invisibility? The human eye cannot register the whole spectrum of light. We cannot see infra-red.
>
> Maybe Nessie's coat has some sort of colour that doesn't show up too good on most people's retinas. That would explain a lot.

Yet it would be wrong to suggest that little has changed. At Loch Ness the heyday of monster-hunting seems to be over. Ironically, the fiftieth anniversary in 1983 of the first eyewitness claims to receive worldwide attention prompted a resurgence of scepticism, and the idea that an unknown creature may lurk in the loch has been subjected to a number of carefully researched and skilfully argued attacks.

At the same time, the ever-optimistic investigators have set out for lake-shores new in pursuit of creatures which, many believe, have survived in their freshwater fastnesses since prehistoric times.

Reports that a monster had been seen rearing up out of the waters of Lake Hanas, China, were investigated by technicians from Xinjiang University in 1980. They travelled to the lake, which is set deep in thickly forested mountains 500 miles north of Urumqi in the Xinjiang Uygur region, and laid bait in the water. All they saw, however, was 'a large red shape', which approached the bait before disappearing back into the depths.

In Canada, in the 1980s, a weird pair of creatures was said to inhabit Saddle Lake and Christina Lake in Alberta. Ray Makowecki, Director of the region's Fish and Wildlife Department, told enquirers:

We've received so many reports of the creatures at both lakes that we've had to take them seriously. There is no obvious and logical explanation.

Besides their heads which are shaped like horses', and their eyes which are the size of saucers, the most astonishing feature is their hair, something like Bo Derek's hair-do in the film *10*. And all of the reports were from trusted and very credible people.

In 1982 a Polish newspaper, *Kurter Polski,* described how a student swimming in Zegrzynski Lake near Warsaw claimed he had been confronted by a beast with 'an enormous slimy black head with rabbit-like ears'. He struck out for the shore at once and when he got there the creature had disappeared, leaving only 'huge ripples' to show where it had been.

A Russian writer, Anatoly Pankov, reported on the hunt for a greyish, long-necked creature apparently seen since the 1950s by several witnesses in Lake Labinkir in the province of Yakutia in Siberia. A group of geologists said it made a sound 'much like a child's cry', while some reindeer-hunters claimed they had watched it coil up out of the water and snaffle a passing bird. Pankov tells of another hunter who took ingenious revenge on the monster after it had swallowed his dog. First he made an animal-skin raft and then piled it high with red-hot coals before pushing it out over the water. The monster duly took the bait and dived away, only to reappear a few moments later 'making terrible sounds'.

There have been the inevitable false alarms. From the town of Alma Ata in Kazakhstan in December 1985 the Soviet news agency Tass cabled the results of an expedition mounted by the Soviet Academy of Science's Institute of Evolutionary Morphology and Ecology of Animals. For years, a monster had been sighted in Lake Kol-Kol. Some eyewitnesses said it was like a dinosaur; others reported that 'a twisty body about 20 metres long emerges above the lake surface time and again'.

In reaching their conclusion, the scientists

refused to be distracted by the colourful accounts of the locals. 'The lake is connected to underground cavities by mud-covered cracks,' they reported. 'When the mud is washed away and water rushes down, large whirlpools appear on the water surface – the traces of the unknown beast.'

In West Germany in July 1982 bathers in a flooded gravel pit near Augsburg were horrified to realize that they were sharing the water with a writhing serpentine creature. The police were duly called and arrested a boa constrictor. How had it got into the pit? Answer: It a was very hot day and the snake's thoughtful owner had simply brought his pet along for a swim.

The case for the existence of a monster in Lake Champlain in the United States of America, was boosted in 1984 by the publication of a book called *Champ – Beyond the Legend*. Its author, Joseph Zarzynski, has collected more than 200 eyewitness reports which suggest that a mysterious creature may live in the lake. There is certainly plenty of room for a monster to hide: Lake Champlain is 109 miles long and runs from the Canadian border through Vermont and down to New York State.

Zarzynski has assembled an impressive number of nineteenth-century sightings. For example, a Captain Crum claimed to have seen 'Champ' from his boat in Bulwagga Bay in July 1819. He said it was almost 200 ft (60 m) long and held its head more than 15 ft (4.5 m) above the water. In August 1871 passengers on the steamer *Curlew* off Barber Point watched through a telescope as a huge and mysterious creature ploughed through the water 'at railroad speed'. Ten years later a steamboat pilot, Mr Warren Rockwell, took a pot shot at an 'animal' from the rear deck of his vessel near Swanton, Vermont. The

creature made itself scarce. In 1880 a Dr Brigham of Bedford, Quebec, and a friend had spotted 'portions of a strange monster's body fully 20 ft long, head as large as a flour barrel, eyes with greenish tinge' in Missisquoi Bay.

In the 1960s Avril Trudeau and a friend reported seeing something with 'an ostrich- or duck-like face' off Maquam shore, Vermont. This is just one of many accounts from this century. Earlier, in 1951, Mrs Theresa Megargee shot at something 'more 30 ft rather than 20 ft long' opposite Valcour Island, New York. She was not convinced it was an unknown creature – it might have been an Atlantic sturgeon – but she let it have the full force of 'an old, octagon-barreled .30-40 Winchester rifle' just in case. She told Zarzynski: 'At the time, I thought my beautiful baby might one day be a tempting "hors d'oeuvre", and I was a protective young mother.' In August 1981 Claude Van Kleeck and others were in a boat in Bulwagga Bay when they apparently saw a creature 'not less than 50 ft long, at least as wide as a 55 gallon barrel', while in May 1984, Anna Gagne was treated to more than one sighting off Popasquash Island.

From his collection of eyewitness reports, Zarzynski has built up a composite picture of the monster:

> Champ is approximately 15–30 feet in length . . . It is dark or black in colour with some colour differentiations possibly due to age or sex. Champ has a snake-like head with two horns or ears, a mouth and teeth, and a possible mane or fringe/ridge on its head and neck. Due to the infrequency of land sightings, there is no indication as to any or the number of flippers, but several eyewitnesses have observed a tail off the body. Champ has the ability to dive and swim at considerable speeds and can hold its head erect for a lengthy time. Weight is

'Champ's' champion, Joseph Zarzynski, uses every available technological tool – like this sonar unit – in his search for the Lake Champlain monster.

difficult to estimate, however, based on size descriptions, a body weight of several tons wouldn't be out of reason.

Zarzynski's prize piece of evidence is a photograph purporting to show Champ, taken on 5 July 1977. Anthony and Sandra Mansi were at the lakeside near St Albans, Vermont, when, they claim, a dinosaur-like head popped out of the water. Anthony quickly passed a Kodak Instamatic to Sandra before rushing off to rescue her two children who were paddling nearby. Sandra managed to take one snapshot. The picture is puzzling. It apparently shows a hump and what Zarzynski terms 'an appendage', presumably either a neck and head or a tail.

Analysis by two scientists failed to resolve all the questions. Dr B. Roy Frieden of the Optical Sciences Center, University of Arizona, was satisfied that the photograph had not been tampered with and that it was neither a montage nor a superimposition. Examination, using the latest technical methods, including computer enhancement, told him virtually nothing more. But he did have doubts. A woman who had once lived near the lake pointed out a curious brownish streak in the picture. Was it, she wondered, a sand bar? Frieden took another look. 'I think it's a real detail in the picture,' he concluded. This had 'interesting implications', for, if the streak *was* a sand bar,

Sandra Mansi's photograph taken from the shores of Lake Champlain in 1977. Does it show the monster?

'then there is a distinct possibility that the object was put there by someone, either by the people who took the photo or by the people who were fooling them, because you could simply walk out on such a sand bar and tow the object behind you and hide behind it as you made it rise out of the water and so forth.'

Dr Paul LeBlond, an oceanographer from the University of British Columbia, offered a quite different interpretation. He looked carefully at the waves on the water shown in the photograph and wrote:

> As waves travel into shallower water, they slow down, steepen, and eventually break. If the paler area corresponded to the presence of a shallow sand bank, one would expect the waves to be modified, and particularly to break more often there than elsewhere. This is not the case, and it seems more reasonable to attribute the different appearance of that part of the lake surface to reflection of light from the overhead clouds.

Resolution of the argument is hampered by the fact that the Mansis, who were strangers to the area, are unable to remember exactly where they were on the lakeside when the picture was taken.

In the meantime, the indefatigable Zarzynski continues in his quest, gathering further eyewitness testimony, probing the depths with sonar and underwater video, in the hope of establishing once and for all that the creature he has pursued for more than a decade really does exist.

Not everyone gives him much chance. Michel Meurger of the Institut Métapsychique International in Paris, and Claude Gagnon, Professor of Philosophy at Montreal University, began to collect claimed sightings of monsters in Canadian lakes in 1981. Meurger told readers of the *Fortean Times*

that, by February 1983, their work had revealed 'the surprising number of fifty mon-
strous lakes, and we had only covered a small
part of our map!' A detailed examination of
the eyewitness reports left the two investigators unconvinced. The descriptions given
seemed so inconsistent:

> In vain we seek coherence in the details; we
> have a choice of features for each part of the
> body – head, neck, back, tail and appendages.
> Depending upon our cryptozoological theories,
> we can recognize fashionable mammals, accept-
> able saurians, and, for the more conservative,
> comprehensible fishes. The only problem is that
> *everything is available.*

Even in small lakes at least four different
types of monster had allegedly been spotted:
in Saint-François, for example, there were
the 'upturned boat' variety, the 'giant fish',
the 'living trunk' and the 'horse-like head'.
Comments Meurger:

> The lake monsters themselves taunt us with
> elusiveness in their bodies as well as their
> habitats. Their forms melt away like jelly or
> the fauna of dreams.
> It seems impossible that *four* (or more) quite
> different and totally unknown types of large
> animal could co-exist in some Quebecian lakes,
> many of which are of only average size and
> depth. It is difficult to believe that such lakes
> could sustain a viable breeding population of
> each – even the resources of the giant Lake
> Champlain would not be sufficient!'

And he concludes: 'Certainly, my fieldwork
in Quebec seems to indicate that it would be
more promising to study the inhabitants on
the shores of a lake than to probe its murky
waters.'

The watchers on the banks of Loch Ness have
now been under scrutiny for a full half-
century, and they can have drawn little
comfort from a book published to mark the

anniversary in 1983. It bore the bold but
simple title, *The Loch Ness Mystery Solved.*
Authors Ronald Binns and R. J. Bell are
veterans of monster investigations in Scottish lochs, but the revelations in their book
make it abundantly clear that they no longer
believe in the existence of such a creature in
Loch Ness. In 220 pages, many of the accepted 'facts' about the monster are enter-
tainingly challenged, and the book should
certainly be read in full by anyone planning
an expedition to Loch Ness. Here are a couple
of examples of Binns' and Bell's well-argued
'demolition jobs':

The first concerns the idea, much loved by
Nessie's 'biographers', that eyewitness accounts of monster sightings can be traced far
back into history. Binns and Bell decided to
go back to the original sources of these tales,
and what they found convinced them that
'under scrutiny, the legends of Loch Ness all
vanish into thin air'.

For example, a neolithic carved stone
found near the loch is said to portray the
monster, when in fact it carries a Pictish
design common throughout Scotland. Frequently quoted references to sightings in
1520, 1771 and 1885 come from what the
authors call 'an eccentric letter which appeared in *The Scotsman* on 20 October 1933'.
They add that the letter-writer 'failed to
supply either his address or any specific references to the chronicles or publications
wherein his weird and wonderful stories
could be found'. References to a Loch Ness
monster in the works of a Greek historian
called Dio Cassius, who wrote a history of
Rome in about AD 200, or to an article apparently containing a woodcut of the creature in
the Atlanta *Constitution* for November 1896
turn out not to exist. Even St Columba's
encounter with a 'water beast' in the River

Below: Alex Campbell, water bailiff of Loch Ness, part-time journalist and monster-spotter *extraordinaire*.

Ness, reported in a life of the saint written in A D 565, is persuasively dismissed on the grounds that the *River* Ness is some way from the loch and is separated from it by another lake; the 'water beast' is merely one of a cast of many obviously mythical creatures introduced into the story to show that Columba possessed magical powers.

The authors' second target is a man known to generations of monster-seekers. For decades, Alex Campbell was the water bailiff of Loch Ness, employed by the local Fisheries Board. A mesmeric raconteur and therefore much sought-after by television programme makers and journalists, Campbell claimed to have seen the monster no less than eighteen times, and Binns and Bell aptly dub him 'the self-appointed high priest of the loch's mysteries, always at hand with advice and inspiration for new devotees of his fabulous beast'. They reveal that Campbell's role in the Loch Ness monster story has been underestimated. Campbell was not only the water bailiff; he was also a part-time journalist, filing stories from the Fort Augustus end of the loch for the two local papers, the *Inverness Courier* and the *Northern Chronicle*. The first monster report to capture national attention – the sighting by Mr and Mrs John Mackay of Drumnadrochit in April 1933 – can be traced to his colourful pen.

Binns and Bell point out that it makes curious reading, for the article is strikingly lacking in journalistic objectivity. Indeed, it reads as though it has been written by someone determined to convince his readers that they should share his passionate belief in the existence of the monster. The authors of *The Loch Ness Mystery Solved* also express surprise at the sheer number of Campbell's claimed sightings, their elaborately lurid detail, the fact that he was one of the very few

who claimed to have seen Nessie at close range, and that there was a 'curious absence' of any objective evidence in the way of photographs to back up his tales. Most telling of all, however, are their revelations about Campbell's account of his 'best' sighting. It was a story he loved to tell, and it duly made the pages of *Arthur C. Clarke's Mysterious World*:

> I heard the sound of two trawlers coming through the canal from the West. Suddenly there was this upsurge of water right in front of the canal entrance. I was stunned. I shut my eyes three times to make sure I was not imagining things – the head and the huge humped body were perfectly clear. I knew right away that the creature was scared because of its behaviour. The head was twisting about frantically. It was the thud, thud of the engines that was the reason for its upset. As soon as the bow of the first trawler came within my line of vision, that's when it was in its line of vision too, and it vanished out of sight, gone. I

estimated the length of the body as 30 ft at least, the height of the head and neck above water level as 6 ft, and the skin was grey.

Campbell gave several different dates for this episode, which does not help his case, but far more damning is the fact that the loquacious water bailiff apparently explained it away in a letter to his employers in 1933. First, he describes what he saw:

I noticed a strange object on the surface about six hundred yards from where I stood. It seemed to be about 30 feet long, and what I took to be the head was fully 5 feet above the surface of the Loch. The creature, if such it was, and at the time I felt certain of it, seemed to be watching two drifters passing out of the Canal and into Loch Ness; and, whether it was due to imagination or not, I could have sworn that it kept turning its head and also its body very quickly, in much the same way as a cormorant does on rising to the surface. I saw this for fully a minute, then the object vanished as if it had sunk out of sight.

The explanation followed:

Last Friday I was watching the Loch at the same place and about the same time of day. The weather was almost identical – practically calm and the sun shining through a hazy kind of mist. In a short time something very like what I have described came into my line of vision and at roughly the same distance from where I stood.

But the light was improving all the time, and in a matter of seconds I discovered that what I took to be the Monster was nothing more than a few cormorants, and what seemed to be the head was a cormorant standing in the water and flapping its wings, as they often do. The other cormorants, which were strung out in a line behind the leading bird, looked in the poor light and at first glance just like the body or humps of the Monster, as it has been described by various witnesses.

But the most important thing was, that owing to the uncertain light the bodies of the birds were magnified out of proportion to their proper size. This mirage-like effect I have often seen on Loch Ness, although not exactly in the same form as I have just described.

Does it matter that Campbell, in his enthusiasm for his beloved loch and the monster he had done so much to make famous, may have been guilty of the fault, known to many a journalist, of not letting the facts spoil a good story? It may do, for Campbell's first accounts conditioned visitors to the loch to expect to find evidence of a monster there. Commander Rupert Gould, a noted writer and broadcaster on mysterious phenomena and one of the original investigators of the monster reports in 1933, saw the danger: 'It is quite true that if you are eagerly on the look-out for something and expect to see it, you are very likely to be misled by anything bearing even a faint resemblance to the thing which you expect to see.'

So how do Binns and Bell interpret the hundreds of monster sightings? Since they believe that no single theory can explain them all, they offer quite a variety, among them swimming deer ('horned monsters'), otters (at least two of the rare sightings on land turn out to contain, they say, 'only a marginally exaggerated description of an otter'), floating tar barrels (left over from road improvements), tree trunks ('single-humped monsters'), and wakes of the many boats that criss-cross the loch. Other sightings they ascribe to mirages. Alex Campbell was far from being the only person to have seen them: the authoritative six-volume *Bathymetrical Survey of the Scottish Fresh-Water Lochs,* published in 1910, devotes a special section to mirages seen at Loch Ness. The authors of *The Loch Ness Mystery Solved* add that the summer of 1933 was particularly fine – ideal mirage conditions.

The 'Surgeon's Photograph' as it is usually published. The close-up provides no clues for estimating the size of the 'monster'.

Binns and Bell were not the only investigators at work. In April 1984 perhaps the most formidable of them all, Steuart Campbell of Edinburgh, published an article in the *British Journal of Photography* to mark – in a devastatingly back-handed way – the fiftieth anniversary of the taking of one of the most famous of all Loch Ness monster photographs. Known as 'the surgeon's picture', it had been snapped in April 1934 by a London gynaecologist called Robert Kenneth Wilson.

Wilson's story was that he had been driving along the lochside road early in the morning, when he noticed 'a considerable commotion on the surface, some distance out from the shore, perhaps two or three hundred yards out. When I watched it for perhaps a minute or so, something broke surface and I saw the head of some strange animal rising out of the water. I hurried to the car for my camera . . .' He said he took four photographs, but two of them turned out to be blank when they were developed by the local chemist. One was bought by a newspaper, which published only the section showing the 'monster'.

Steuart Campbell managed to locate the full print, by then extremely tattered, and looked carefully at both pictures. Wilson had claimed that he had been 'some hundred feet above the loch' when the pictures were taken and that the 'monster' had been 'between 150 and 200 yards from the shore'. But using the prints, and calculating the angle from which the pictures must have been taken, Campbell calculated that Wilson had, in fact, been very much nearer the water than he had said. Campbell also showed that the 'monster' must be only 28 in (0.70 m) high, observing, 'That is a rather small monster!'

Finally, Campbell suggested that the photographs probably show an otter. In one – the frame usually published – its tail is visible; in the other, its head. Commented Campbell: 'It can hardly be an accident that this second picture, which might have revealed the true nature of the object, is out of focus.' There seemed, in short, to be a distinct element of hoax about the whole thing. This revealing analysis shook one of the main photographic pillars of support for the existence of the Loch Ness monster.

Campbell later moved on to a re-examination of the most famous piece of motion picture evidence, the so-called 'Dinsdale film'. This was taken on 23 April 1960 by Tim Dinsdale, an aeronautical engineer who was on a lone investigation of the monster. On the last morning of his trip, Dinsdale was in his car, rolling down the road near the Foyers Hotel, when he saw a puzzling object about three-quarters of a mile out in the loch. It was large, dappled, and 'a distinct mahogany colour'. Dinsdale slammed on the brakes, jumped out and located the object with his binoculars. Now it looked like a living creature – with humps. He started to film, pausing only to rewind the motor of his clockwork cine camera. With only a few feet of film left, he made a desperate dash to the lochside in the hope of a closer shot, but, to

his exasperation, by the time he got there the object had disappeared from view.

Shortly afterwards, with good scientific principles in mind, Dinsdale persuaded the owner of the Foyers Hotel to take a dinghy with an outboard motor on to the water and to follow the course taken by the mysterious object. The two sequences could then be compared.

Later, the film was analyzed by experts at JARIC (the Joint Air Reconnaissance Intelligence Centre), a leading British photographic interpretation unit. The centre's Report Number 66/1 set the seal on the mystery, for the experts opined that the object was not a boat – it had been moving too fast to have been a dinghy with an outboard motor, and was not painted in the bright colours of a power boat. The report's conclusion brought joy to monster-hunters: 'One can presumably rule out the idea that it is any sort of submarine vessel for various reasons which leaves the conclusion that it is probably an animate object.'

Some twenty years later, in the *Photographic Journal*, Steuart Campbell took another look at the report, and discovered what he took to be a crucial flaw. Dinsdale had said that he had not only paused during filming but had also had to stop so that he could wind up his camera. Campbell suggested that he had done this at least twice. This of course meant that the film did not show one continuous sequence. JARIC, however, appeared not to have taken this into account and, by mistakenly contracting the timescale, had reached the wrong conclusion about the speed at which the object had been travelling. When the pauses between shots had been added to the overall timings, the object and the hotel-owner's dinghy, which Dinsdale had filmed for com-

The tattered remains of the full print of the 'Surgeon's Photograph'. The 'monster' can now be seen to be far smaller than the cropped version suggests.

parison, were found to have been moving at a similar rate. Campbell therefore arrived at this no-nonsense verdict: 'The only mystery about the film is why it should ever have been thought that it showed anything other than a boat, and why JARIC did not reach the right conclusion.'

The arguments, of course, will continue, as they have done now for the past half-century, in the pages of learned journals, in books, in the lochside pubs far into the chilly Highland nights, and on the shores of the great lake itself during long, hopeful vigils. The monster-hunters, assailed as they increasingly are by the carefully researched doubts of the sceptics, can bask in one certainty: the world wants Loch Ness to have a monster. While there is a chance, however faint, that such a creature may exist, the search is sure to go on.

A traditional view of the Kraken's power to
threaten a ship.

5.

Of Monsters and Mermaids

The terrors of the deep are genuine enough. In 1985 a large shark was killed in the Gulf of Thailand. In its stomach were the skulls of two men, 'adults of Caucasian origin'. The same year, sharks, unusually, started taking surfers off the coast of California. The theory emerged that people wearing black wet suits look like seals, one of the sharks' food sources. In 1986 in Kiribati – once the Gilbert Islands – local fishermen watched in horror as a creature with tentacles grabbed first one and then another of their colleagues and dragged them down to die in the depths.

Recent years have seen some of the mysteries of the deep resolved, others rendered all the more intriguing. Some fears have been allayed. The sea snake, with the deadliest venom in the world, seems to reserve its lethal powers for fellow marine creatures and hardly ever attacks man. Other horrors have been reinforced – not least sharks.

The incident in Kiribati added another makeweight to the balance of evidence which now suggests that there may indeed be truly giant octopuses lurking in the vast biosphere of the sea. There is room enough. Not only does the sea cover nearly three-quarters of the earth's surface, but its great depths mean that there is perhaps 300 times as much living space than is to be found on the plateaus of earth's dry land. Reminders of our ignorance are regularly delivered.

In 1984 the fishing vessel *Helga* netted a megamouth shark off Catalina Island, Cali-

fornia – only the second member ever seen of what is now established as an entirely new species. It now floats in a tank of ethanol at the Los Angeles Museum of Natural History – a 15-ft (4.5-m) -long symbol of how little we know of the sea. And the marine biologists regularly outline the huge area of darkness in which they operate. Biologist Malcolm Clarke, studying sperm whales, found in their stomachs not only huge quantities of squid – up to 30,000 squid jaws in one whale's gut – but species rarely or never caught in the plethora of nets and devices which the scientists use to prospect the sea. Yet the weight of these unknown creatures eaten by whales each year, he calculated, exceeds that of the entire human race put together. The squid, some of them very large to judge by their beaks, must exist in their millions, yet many species rarely fall into the hands of man; there must be many more which man has never seen.

The Giant Octopus

In 1984 a weird series of incidents off the coast of Bermuda gave a hint that the lair of the giant octopus may have been found. It has been clear that this creature is not merely a chimera ever since the day in 1896 when an enormous carcass was washed up on the beach at St Augustine in Florida. The main part of the body weighed around 7 tons and was 18 ft (5.5 m) long by 10 ft (3 m) across. A local naturalist, Dr De Witt Webb,

Below: the *Helga*'s megamouth shark, caught off California in 1984.

measured two of the tentacles, though he thought they were only stumps, at 23 ft (7 m) and 32 ft (10 m). His view then was that he was dealing with an octopus of daunting proportions – perhaps 200 ft (60 m) across. His photographs leave no room to doubt the bulk of the animal, but what has sustained modern confidence in the veracity of his attribution was the happy coincidence that a piece of the animal's flesh was preserved in the Smithsonian Institution in Washington, DC. This meant that in 1963 Dr Joseph Gennaro could make a histological analysis. He concluded that the tissue was not from a squid or a whale and was probably from an octopus.

But the mystery remains: could such gigantic creatures really exist when the largest octopus otherwise known to man is a mere 23 ft (7 m)?

In the summer of 1984 a Bermuda trawler owner, John P. Ingham, was working on what he hoped would be a profitable theory. He thought that very large – and commercially attractive – shrimps and crabs might be found, if he could only get traps down to

1,000 fathoms or so – more than 6,000 ft (1,800 m) – off the Bermuda shelf. The theory was working: he had brought up ½-lb (500-gm) shrimps, and crabs 2 ft (60 cm) across. Ingham now proceeded to construct really strong traps built of ¼- and ⅜-in iron rods, braced with 2-in (5-cm) tree staves. They measured between 6 and 8 ft (1.8 and 2.4 m) square by 4 ft (1.2 m) deep. The traps were lowered and raised by winch from John Ingham's 50-ft (15-m) boat, *Trilogy*.

By the beginning of September Ingham had already had a couple of worrying incidents. First he lost a trap after a sudden strain on the line. There was nothing obvious to explain it. Then, a few days later, on 3 September, the crew were hauling up a new pot and had reached about 300 fathoms when they felt the line being pulled out. There was a series of jerks, and once again the line parted. On 19 September 1984 Mr Ingham had a trap set at 480 fathoms – around 2,800 ft (850 m) down. This time, even with the full force of the winch, they could not break the pot clear of the bottom at all. *Trilogy* is equipped with a sophisticated type of sonar known as a chromascope, and Skipper Ingham went inside to use it. He set the 'scope on what is known as 'split bottom mode'. There, clearly outlined on the ocean floor, was a pyramid-like shape, measurable on the chromascope as fully 50 ft (15 m) high: something was surrounding their trap. Ingham and his crew decided not to force the issue this time. They would settle down and wait, with the rope snubbed as tight as possible on the winch. After about twenty minutes, Ingham suddenly had the eerie feeling that the boat was starting to move – that it was being towed.

Again he went inside to check his array of navigation instruments. The positions given

Part of the carcass of a giant octopus which
came ashore at Santa Cruz in 1925.

Below: John P. Ingham claimed he could feel thumps
travelling along the rope to his boat, as if some creature
at the other end was walking along the ocean floor.

by the Loran are extremely precise. The instrument confirmed his view. The boat was
moving steadily south at a speed of about 1
knot. After about 500 yards, whatever was
towing the *Trilogy* decided to change direction and turned inshore. A short distance
further on it abruptly turned again. By now
Ingham was convinced that some creature
had hold of his pot and was steadily advancing, trap, 50-ft boat and all, towards some
private destination. At one point Mr Ingham
put his hand on the rope near the water line.
'I could distinctly feel thumps like something
was walking and the vibrations were travelling up the rope.' The 50-ft sonar lump, the
peregrinations of the boat, the thumps, the
previous lost traps – Ingham was now convinced that he was in the grip of some truly
gigantic sea creature.

Suddenly the creature appeared to let go.

Below: Ingham's boat *Trilogy* was towed by some unknown force.

The rope became slack and the crew had no trouble hauling up the trap. It was bent on one side and the top had been stoved in.

Neither cameras nor underwater scanners operated by scientists have accompanied Mr Ingham, but the circumstances point firmly to an octopus: a creature on the ocean floor with the power to retain a trap against a large ship's winch; an accumulation of bite-size shrimp and crab – kindly if regretfully arranged by Mr Ingham; the location off the Bermuda shelf: all lead inexorably to the idea of a large octopus. No other creature known or imagined could conceivably give such a show of strength in such circumstances. Perhaps the homeland of the great creature which was so mysteriously washed up almost a century ago in Florida has now at last been located.

Mermaids

Recent research has solved one of the world's other sea mysteries, the mermaid stories. Two Canadian scientists from Winnipeg, Drs Lehn and Schroeder, ascribed visions of mermaids to a precise optical illusion. They knew

that sightings of mermaids could be traced back to medieval Norse texts, such as *The King's Mirror,* which were otherwise very accurate in their descriptions of sea creatures. Only the mermaid and the kraken – the sea monster – are not recognized by today's marine biologists. The author of *The King's Mirror* gives a very vivid and precise description of a merman:

> This monster is tall and of great size and rises straight out of the water. It has shoulders like a man's but no hands. Its body apparently grows narrower from the shoulders down, so that the lower down it has been observed, the more slender it has seemed to be. But no one has ever seen how the lower end is shaped. No one has ever observed it closely enough to determine whether its body has scales like a fish or skin like a man. Whenever the monster has shown itself, men have always been sure that a storm would follow.

The author then describes its mate, the mermaid, which has breasts, hair, large webbed hands and a tail like a fish. This description tallies closely with a creature in the north Pacific, known to Japanese chroniclers as *umibohzu,* or the priest of the sea.

Lehn and Schroeder suggested that in the cold northern waters, the warmer air which predicates a storm would mix in a layer over the sea, creating a swirling mass of air of changing temperature which could act as a distorting lens, exaggerating the height but not the width of an object. Seen through this natural hall of mirrors, the head of a walrus or the top of a whale could assume the lowering shape of a merman or mermaid. It was only a theory, though tested through a computer programme developed for ray-tracing. But the two doctors finally got a chance to prove their point when one spring day the atmospheric conditions on Lake Winnipeg

In the nineteenth century the hypothesis was advanced that manatee was a possible source of the mermaid stories.

Below: Lehn and Schroeder's 'mermaid' on Lake Winnipeg.

seemed perfect: on land it was a hot day (28°C) but some thin ice still remained on the lake. They went out in a boat and, sure enough, a mermaid appeared – and stayed long enough to be photographed. It was convincing enough to make a modern mariner believe he had met a siren. In fact it was a boulder sticking out of the water half a mile away.

This new proof of the accuracy of the Norse seamen in their observations seems to dispose of the Atlantic mermaid at least; though

it suggests that their description of the great kraken – now the one unrecognized phenomenon in *The King's Mirror* – might also be frighteningly accurate.

But the explanation of a cold-water mirage hardly sufficed for the vivid encounters repeatedly described in the tropical waters of Papua New Guinea.

Roy Wagner, Head of the Anthropology Department of the University of Virginia, had heard tales of the *ri* back in 1979. A local magistrate told him he had met a *ri* near a reef while on a fishing expedition off New Ireland. The creature had risen from the sea and stared at him. It had a monkey-like face rather than a human one. As it went on staring, the magistrate flung his spear at it. 'But I couldn't make up my mind whether to hit him or not, so I threw it crookedly. You would expect it to be frightened off, but no. It just surfaced farther on, and stared at me again.'

Wagner collected a number of similar stories, and then one day in Ramat Bay, he himself saw a long dark shape, which the locals said was a *ri* or mermaid. All the descriptions agreed that the *ri* had long dark hair on its head, was light-skinned and that the females had breasts like women. Wagner was sufficiently intrigued to organize an expedition in 1983 with Richard Greenwell of the International Society of Cryptozoology. This only added to the mystery, for they did indeed observe at relatively close quarters a large creature rolling and blowing on the surface and then disappearing for ten minutes or more beneath the water – behaviour which did not tally with that of any known creature of such size. The *ri* clearly existed, but it remained the *ri* – an unknown creature, and still a mermaid to the Papuans.

Two years later a much more lavishly equipped expedition set out in the 65-ft (20-m) Australian dive boat, *Reef Explorer*, with side scan sonar and video cameras, not to mention ship-to-shore telephones and air-conditioned cabins. When they got to Nokon Bay, New Ireland, they saw an animal rolling and playing on the surface. It clearly had no dorsal fin but seemed to have flukes. At that point a local villager, Tom Omar, came canoeing out to them. This was the *ri* or *ilkai*, he pronounced. The female, he said, had a woman's breasts, hair and hands. Indeed, there was a family of them in the bay – male, female and child, he reported.

During the next ten days the captain of the *Reef Explorer*, Kerry Piesch, and other members of the expedition managed to get near the creature with underwater video and still cameras. One photo was clear and unmistakable: the animal was a dugong – a rare but not unknown sea creature. The theory that the *ri* was a dugong had been considered and dismissed, as the *ri*'s behaviour was quite unlike anything hitherto reported about dugongs. In particular, it was thought that the dugong could dive for only a minute or so at a time; the New Ireland animal was under water for upwards of ten minutes. But as the pictures and the video accumulated, there was little room for doubt. Then came a sad conclusion. One morning the villagers were seen pulling a large creature out of the water. It turned out to be a dead female. No breasts, no hair, and undoubtedly a dugong. She had been shot by a high-powered rifle. No culprit was found, though the villagers blamed neighbours from the next bay. The corpse, laid out on the beach at Nokon Bay, effectively ended the hunt for the Papuan mermaid. But it was not hard to see how that strange body, with its hand-like flukes, cavorting out of the water

Below: The dead 'merman' turns out to be a dugong.

in the haze of a tropical sea, might well answer the pervasive and attractive myth of men and girls cast or lured into the ocean and transmuted into mermen and mermaids to fascinate mariners for centuries past.

The Kraken

If the mermaid seems to vanish into the mist of imagination, the classic sea monster seems as persistent as ever. Many of the sightings round the British Isles now seem ascribable to the wonderful leathery turtle. This huge creature, as big as a mini car and weighing perhaps 800 lb (360 kilos), now seems to be more common in British waters than was previously thought, for it is born thousands of miles away in the Caribbean or even

Malaysia. Virtually nothing is known of its journeys across the oceans, but it seems unlikely that it would intentionally venture into the chill waters of the North Atlantic.

In 1985, however, another great leathery turtle came ashore near Mousehole in Cornwall. It was nearly 7 ft (2.5 m) long and weighed just under 7 hundredweight. It had apparently choked on a plastic bag, mistaking it for the jelly fish which are its principal food source. Many of the descriptions of classic British sea monsters, such as the Soay monster, suggest the leather back turtle as a convincing explanation. But no one has yet proposed a satisfactory solution to the traditional sea monster with horse's head and humps, which has been seen by seamen

The leathery turtle: as big as a small car.

and shore watchers all over the world and seems as common as ever.

At least six people saw the Stinson Beach monster north of San Francisco one after-noon in October 1983. Matt Ratto was a mem-ber of a construction crew working on the highway. They had binoculars which were apparently used for observing frolics on the beach during their lunch breaks. However, this time they were at hand for more serious viewing when one of the crew called up on the two-way radio and told Ratto to look out to sea. The mystery animal was only 100 yards off shore and about a quarter of a mile away when Ratto focused on it. It was being followed by a large flock of birds and about two dozen sea lions. Ratto and his fellow crew members all agreed that the creature was about 100 ft (30 m) long – they had the sea lions with which to compare it. Ratto said: 'There were three bends like humps and they

rose straight up. Then the head came up to look around.' Truck driver Steve Bjora thought it looked like a huge eel. 'The sucker was going 45 to 50 miles an hour. It was clipping. It was boogeying.'

Safety inspector Marlene Martin of the California Department of Transport appar-ently told her family it was the biggest thing she had ever seen in her life: 'It made Jaws look like a baby.' A teenager on the beach below, Roland Curry, also saw the animal, and reported that it was his second sighting within a week. The first time, it was visible for only about thirty seconds and the head came up for a couple of seconds before the animal dived. Later the same week a surfer, Young Hutchinson, reported that a sea ser-pent had surfaced within 10 ft (3 m) of his surfboard off the Santa Ana River: 'At first I thought it was a whale, but I've seen a lot of whales and it didn't look the same at all. The skin texture wasn't the same and there were no dorsal fins. In fact it was like a long black eel. It was really moving. We got the hell out of there and paddled for the shore.'

The local scientists all offered the usual explanations of pilot whales and porpoises in a line jumping from the water. But these do not seem adequate for a creature viewed for some time by a group of people, one of whom had binoculars, and then at very close quarters by an apparently level-headed surfer. In the chronicles of sea monsters, Stinson Beach, 1983, seems a hard one to explain away.

A more enigmatic recent report comes from Iceland. Two bird-watchers, Olafur Lafsson and Julius Asgeirsson, were on the beach twenty miles north of Reykjavik, when they saw two creatures emerging from the sea and gambolling about on the beach. Asgeirsson said: 'They were larger than horses, they moved about like dogs, but they swam like seals.' The animals soon went back into the water, leaving behind tracks in the sand. 'The footprints were larger than those of horse hoofs and split like those of a cloven-footed animal, but with three cloves instead of two.' No explanation beyond the shrouded visions of the old Icelandic sagas has yet appeared.

One putative source for the eel-like sea monster has been thoroughly discredited by recent research. Over the last century a few examples of giant eel larvae have been trawled out of the oceans. One captured by the round-the-world *Dana* expedition in 1930 was nearly 6 ft (2 m) long. Comparisons with other eel larvae suggested that it might grow into a serpent of mammoth proportions if it progressed in similar fashion. There was speculation about giant eels of up to 150 ft (45 m), which might well fit the bill as sea

monsters. However, Dr David Smith of the University of Texas has shown that not only do the giant eel larvae not go on growing, they actually get shorter when they transmute into a fish, becoming spiny eels of only 2 or 3 ft (60 to 90 cm) in length.

Mermaids and giant eels have receded in recent years; the giant octopus seems a little closer; but the regular surprises, from the coelacanth to the megamouth, indicate that the huge, barely explored territories of the great oceans are well capable of retaining many secrets even in the age of high-powered submarine technology.

Arthur C. Clarke comments:

A few years ago an oil company engineer passing through Sri Lanka told me a story which makes a splendid sequel to our programme 'Monsters of the Deep' (Chapter 4 of *Arthur C. Clarke's Mysterious World*).

Everyone must have seen pictures of the enormous oil-rigs which are used for ocean drilling; some of them are as big as skyscrapers. Well, it seems that one of these rigs had a problem. The divers couldn't go down to inspect it because it was covered by an octopus! I could not discover exactly – or even approximately – what percentage of the rig was so ornamented. Of course, objects are magnified under water, and the first diver down probably did not stop to make accurate measurements.

As an inoperative rig costs a few hundred thousand dollars a day in lost revenue, the oil company, sadly but understandably, did not call for marine scientists to come and examine this splendid specimen whenever it was convenient. They shooed it away with carefully calibrated underwater explosions – without, I hope, giving it a headache.

Some new light has also been thrown on

Below: Steller's sea cow: there have been reports that it still survives in the Soviet Pacific.

the giant squid (genus *Architeuthis*). These creatures of the deep apparently cannot survive long in warm waters because their blood will not transport oxygen efficiently at more than 10°C. So if you ever meet one on the surface in tropical waters (*vide* the chapter 'Squid' in *Moby Dick*), it is almost certainly dying. I would not suggest that even the most ardent conservationist attempt mouth-to-beak resuscitation.

Turning to less fearsome sea monsters (not that I would care to meet one when snorkling peacefully along the reef), I am grateful to Michel Raynal of Narbonne, France, for an item about the possible survival of Steller's sea cow. The translation is so delightful that it would be a pity to correct it:

Where are you, Steller's sea cow?*

'You know,' – told me once Ivan Nikiforovich Chechulin, projectionist of the Karaginskaya culture and propaganda team – 'in summer 1976, I took part in some operations during the salmon fishing season in the Anapkinskaya Bay. A team of sealers of the collective farm "Tumgutum" consisted of the local population, namely koryaks and Olutorsky Gulf inhabitants. Everybody took part in the fishery from their childhood.

Once, just after a heavy storm we noticed an unknown animal on a tidal belt, its skin was dark, its tail was forked like that one of the whale, the extremities of the animal were flippers. There were slightly noticed outlines of some round ribs. We approached the animal, touched it and were surprised as its head beared an unusual form and its snout was long. None of us has ever seen this animal.

'Perhaps, it was a small seal or a bearded seal, or a Steller's sea-lion' – asked me half-serious, half in joke. 'You don't say that,' Chechulin felt hurt. 'Don't we know? Every one of us took part in the sealing hundred times. Small seal's blubber called by the local population "nymilan" is the best seasoning to "yukola" (local word for the dried and cured salmon) and "tolkusha" (also a local word). All marine animals are known to us.'

I showed several drawings of the Steller's sea cow to Ivan Nikiforovich, the animal whose description was firstly given in 1741 found on the Commander Islands by an eminent naturalist George Wilhelm Steller. Presently, this animal, the sea cow, bears the name of the Steller's sea cow. 'Just the same thing,' – said I. N. Chechulin examining the picture. – 'The same tail, the fore flippers and the head . . . Aren't they left now?' – he asked surprised. 'Not a

single one,' answered me. – 'Though in 1966, a Museum of local lore was created in an Ust-Pakhachinskaya school.'

TINRO scientists became interested in two school exhibits, those were bones of some marine animals. Later on, the scientists published the results of their investigations in a newspaper *Kamchatskaya Pravda* where they paid their attention to the fact that one of those bones appeared to be a bone of a sea cow died about 10 years ago.

For the present, the facts testify to another thing. The Steller's sea cow was fired out by hunters throughout a short term. Inhabiting lagoons in the ashore waters, where it fed on sea algae and eel grass, the Steller's sea cow was a relic and dying animal.

Presently, the skull of the Steller's sea cow is exposed in our Museum. A complete skeleton of the animal is kept in Khabarovsk Museum of local lore.

Kamchatka is studied insufficiently in biological and geographical aspects. There can be found hundreds of areas in our country seldom visited by people and where marine mammals can inhabit easily including the Steller's sea cow. These areas are lagoons, estuaries, lakes with warm water open to the sea.

The opinion of the scientists cannot be considered as a stable one for always. Let it be yet considered that the Steller's sea cow has died out. But . . . to prove it finally, it is necessary to organize a special expedition. There is need to organize a great biological expedition which could start its work already in summer months 1977 throughout all regions of the Kamchatka area with application of the method elaborated by the scientists of the Kamchatka Branch of TINRO.

Undoubtedly, the youth of our area will take an active part in these investigations.

VLADIMIR MALUKOVICH,
senior scientific worker,
Kamchatka Museum of Local Lore.

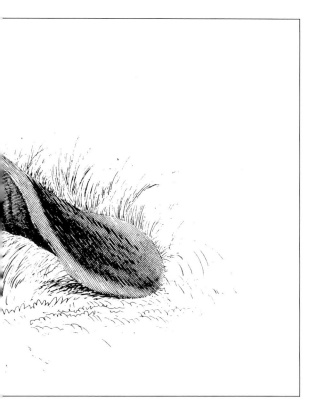

* *Kamchatsky Komsomolets*, Petropavlovsk, January 1977.

Mirages can magically transform workaday objects – here, ferryboats on Puget Sound in the United States. Effects vary according to atmospheric conditions. In the first picture the ship's portholes are elongated and its hull obliterated. In the second, it has disintegrated into a row of floating towers and everything below the bridge has disappeared.

6.

Supernatural Scenes

Fata Morgana

Travellers and explorers love to report curious sights, but some of the things they describe are decidedly stranger than others. Consider these weird tales.

On 24 June 1906 Robert E. Peary, who later claimed to have been the first man to reach the North Pole, spotted through his field glasses, far away on the Arctic horizon, 'the faint white summits of a distant land'. Four days later, according to his diary, from Cape Thomas Hubbard (on the edge of the polar ice) Peary saw the mysterious mountains again, more clearly, to the north-west. 'My heart leaped the intervening miles of ice as I looked longingly at this land, and in fancy I trod its shores, and climbed its summits, even though I knew that that pleasure could be only for another in another season.' Pausing only to name his discovery 'Crocker Land', after his expedition's sponsor, Peary pushed on towards the Pole, convinced that he had found an unknown island or even an uncharted continent. 'Crocker Land' duly appeared on US Hydrographic Office maps; but in 1914 an expedition sent to explore it found not a single trace of Peary's 'discovery'. After a gruelling journey over 150 miles of treacherous Arctic ice, the baffled explorers concluded that 'Crocker Land' simply did not exist.

On the other side of the world, in January 1915, Frank Worsley, captain of Sir Ernest Shackleton's ill-fated ship *Endurance*, noted as he sailed along the Antarctic coast: 'Inshore appears a beautiful dazzling city of cathedral spires, domes and minarets.' And yet, as Worsley well knew, there were no such buildings anywhere in the vast ice deserts surrounding the South Pole.

One August day in the seventeenth century an Italian priest, Father Angelucci, was looking out to sea across the Strait of Messina, which divides the southern tip of Italy from Sicily. Suddenly a shimmering city rose up before him from the midst of the waters. Its pillars, arches and aqueducts were dominated by glittering castles; but within minutes, as Father Angelucci watched in wonder, the magnificent metropolis had vanished.

Almost 300 years later, in the summer of 1929, villagers from Niemiskyliä, central Finland, picking berries in the nearby Osmankisuo swamp, watched in amazement as 'an obscure dark mass' on the north-eastern horizon turned rapidly into 'a most wonderful city with its buildings, squares and streets'. In it, they told a reporter from the *Iisalmen Sanomat* newspaper, they could see people 'on their Sunday morning stroll'. One welltravelled berry-picker identified the city as far-off Berlin, complete with the Unter den Linden and its famous zoo.

In 1852 a Mr M'Farland, in a report to the British Association, described this charming scene; it unfolded as he stood with a party of friends upon a rock at Portbalintrea, Ireland.

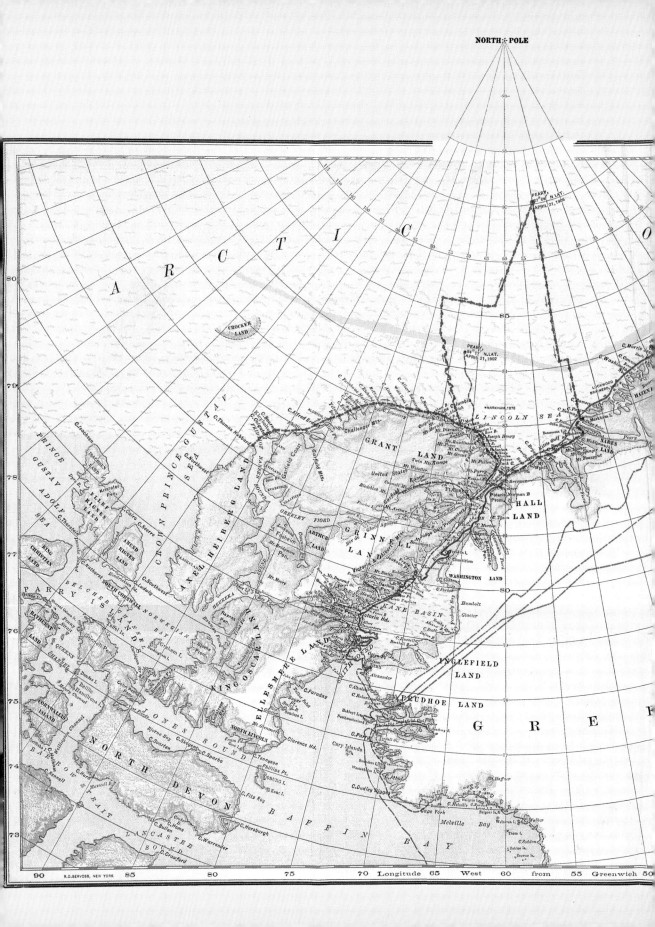

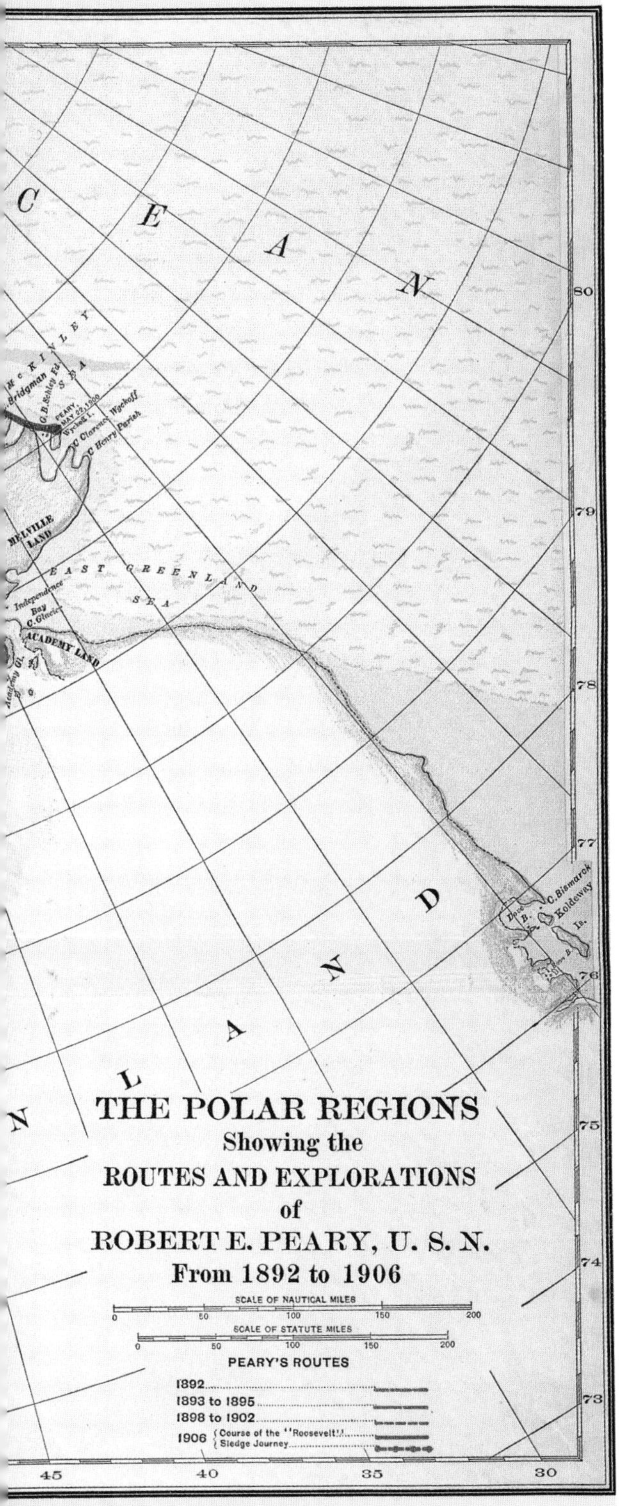

THE POLAR REGIONS
Showing the
ROUTES AND EXPLORATIONS
of
ROBERT E. PEARY, U. S. N.
From 1892 to 1906
SCALE OF NAUTICAL MILES
SCALE OF STATUTE MILES
PEARY'S ROUTES
1892
1893 to 1895
1898 to 1902
1906 Course of the "Roosevelt"
Sledge Journey
MELVILLE LAND
EAST GREENLAND SEA
ACADEMY LAND
Independence Bay
C. Bismarck
Koldeway Is.

'Crocker Land', the country which polar explorer Robert E. Peary claimed to have seen in 1906, featured on maps – until an expedition to the area found that it did not exist.

They

> perceived a small roundish island as if in the act of emerging from the deep, at a distance of a mile from the shore; at first it appeared but as a green field, afterwards it became fringed with red, yellow and blue; whilst the forms of trees, men and cattle rose upon it slowly and successively; and these continued for about a quarter of an hour, distinct in their outlines, shape and colour; the figures, too, seemed to walk across it, or wandered among the trees, the ocean bathed it around, the sun shone upon it from above; and all was fresh, fair, and beautiful, till the sward assumed a shadowy form, and its various objects, mingling into one confused whole, passed away as strangely as they came.

These sights can be explained. The spangled 'cities' of the Antarctic and the Strait of Messina, Mr M'Farland's green and pleasant 'island', Peary's evanescent 'Crocker Land', even the 'Berlin townscape' that so astonished the berry-pickers of the Osmankisuo swamp, were all mirages created by peculiar atmospheric conditions. The travellers were all fooled because these mirages were of a particularly rare and spectacular type, known as the 'Fata Morgana', first accurately described by Father Angelucci and so called because passing Crusaders in the Middle Ages imagined the illusory turrets to be the legendary citadel of Morgan Le Fay, King Arthur's evil sister and a sorceress with a *penchant* for luring sailors to their doom. Simple mirages are common. Drivers are used to seeing what looks like a pool of water ahead of them on a hot, dry road. The pool, of course, does not exist. What they are really seeing is the sky, 'reflected' in the layer of air heated by the ground. This is called an 'inferior mirage'. A 'superior mirage' is caused by a 'reflection' in a layer of warm air high above the ground. The 'Fata

Morgana' is a much weirder and far more complicated type of mirage which occurs when unusual variations in atmospheric temperature create blurred and uneven 'reflections' of the sea.

Phantom Houses

Explanations for other 'phantom scenes' are more difficult to find. Often, after failing to find answers in the natural world, investigators have turned instead to the supernatural, sometimes with unexpected results.

In 1961, in the *Journal of the Society for Psychical Research,* Rosalind Heywood, a prominent investigator of the paranormal, published a curious story told her by a Mr and Mrs Fraser.

Six years earlier, on a Friday evening in November, the Frasers had been driving to Herstmonceux, Sussex, for a weekend in the country. About an hour and a half outside London they spotted a 'lovely old country house' hotel.

> It was covered with lichen, [said Peggy Fraser] and its windows were lighted with a diffused light that speaks of comfort and welcome. There was a gravel drive leading to the porticoed entrance and on the left was built a low sloping-roofed addition with the words 'American Bar' in neon lighting. I can see as if it was only a moment ago the small red-shaded lamps and the bar and bottles and small inviting tables.

To the couple's regret, it was not the hotel where they had booked to stay; but they decided to come back later to sample the *ambience* and drink a nightcap after dinner. But that evening, although the Frasers tried repeatedly to find it again, the quaint hotel seemed to have vanished into thin air. Said Mrs Fraser:

> We talked of nothing else that weekend and

my husband was annoyed, for he felt such a thing should not have happened to him of all people. Since that time we have made many journeys along that road to visit my parents in Hastings and each time we have looked for the hotel but we have never seen it again.

The Frasers' was not the first 'phantom hotel' to have attracted the attention of psychical researchers. In 1933 a Mr and Mrs Clifford Pye were travelling round Cornwall by train and bus. Just outside Boscastle, as the bus paused for a moment to let off a passenger, the couple noticed what they took to be a splendid guest-house surrounded by a beautiful garden full of scarlet geraniums. Chairs and tables were set out on the lawn beneath black and orange umbrellas. Mrs Pye announced that it would be an ideal stopping-place for the night, but at that moment the bus moved on and took them into Boscastle. Later, when they tried to find the guest-house, they could see no trace of it, and further searches in the surrounding area proved fruitless.

The Pyes' story caused some excitement among psychical researchers, for they hailed it as an example of a rare phenomenon, a 'collective hallucination'. These are greatly prized, for the theory goes that while an apparition reported by an individual may exist only in the mind of the beholder, one seen by more than one person may have an objective reality. But the excitement was misplaced, for the Pyes' guest-house and the Frasers' country hotel turned out to exist after all.

Denys Parsons, a member of the Society for Psychical Research, was impressed by the detail of the Frasers' story. He was sure that they must have seen a real building, and confirmed his suspicions by the simple expedient of writing a letter to the East Sussex

Melbourne House, Boscastle: the 'phantom guest-house' identified.

police. The 'phantom hotel', they replied, was a fifteenth-century tea-house called Waldernheath. It stood on the road the Frasers had taken and matched their description almost exactly, except in one inexplicable detail: Waldernheath had no bar and therefore no neon sign.

After a visit to the area and 'an excellent meal in the "non-existent building",' Parsons concluded that the Frasers' powers of observation were clearly first-class – their description of the 'hotel', which they had only seen from a moving car and during a torrential downpour, was accurate in almost every respect. What surprised him was 'their failure to identify a building which turns out to be not only where they thought it was but which tallies with eighteen out of twenty-one of the mental images they associated with it'.

As a result of Denys Parsons' revelations, the file on the Boscastle 'guest-house' was reopened, and an investigation by another member of the Society for Psychical Research, Miss A. M. Scott-Eliott quickly cleared up this case too. After a visit to Boscastle, she reported that the building which the Pyes had glimpsed from the bus did indeed exist. It was called Melbourne House and stood halfway down a steep hill into the village. Miss Scott-Eliott even established that red geraniums had been growing in the garden at the time of the Pyes' visit.

So why had they been unable to find it when they retraced their journey? For one thing, Melbourne House was almost totally hidden behind a hedge and a high wall. It would have been difficult for anyone on foot to see it, especially if they had been going *up* the hill and not down, as the Pyes had done in the bus. Secondly, there had never been any tables with black and orange umbrellas in the garden: these had been outside a café further down the hill and had somehow been 'transported' in the minds of the visitors to the lawn of Melbourne House. Finally, the place was not a guest-house at all, but a private home. Perhaps the Pyes' eagerness to find somewhere pleasant for the night had caused them to assume that it did take guests. Since their first impressions of the place had been so inaccurate, it was hardly surprising that, even if the couple did catch a glimpse of Melbourne House during their search, they failed to associate it with the 'guest-house' that had seemed so welcoming from the bus.

In retrospect, the psychical researchers to whom the stories were first told may have been too uncritical in publishing them as evidence of collective hallucinations, and simple checks like a letter to the local police or a thorough search of the area by an independent investigator would have cleared up the mysteries long before they were enshrined in print. Denys Parsons pointed up the lesson:

> We should indeed accord almost zero value to the type of statement with which accounts of such 'hallucination' cases always conclude: 'Although we searched everywhere and made all sorts of enquiries, the building had vanished without trace.' The layman knows neither how to search nor how to make enquiries . . . Let us resolve to be more fussy about alleged hallucinations.

Today's researchers have taken the hint, and a remarkable story told by two married couples from Dover is being rigorously investigated. This, arguably the strangest of all tales of 'phantom scenery', began in October 1979 while Geoff and Pauline Simpson and Len and Cynthia Gisby were driving through France *en route* to a holiday in Spain. Late in the evening they turned off the *autoroute* near Montélimar and tried to find rooms at a nearby motel, the Ibis, but it was fully booked. Instead they were told to 'try down the road'. A short drive brought them to a long two-storeyed stone building fronting directly on to the highway. The travellers parked their car in the lay-by opposite and Len Gisby went in. He found himself in a large room that housed a bar. Then the *patron* appeared and indicated that there were rooms available (he spoke no English and the travellers knew very little French).

The place struck the couples as quaintly – almost comically – old-fashioned. The bedroom windows were unglazed but fitted with double shutters. The sheets were of heavy calico and there were bolsters instead of pillows. In the bathroom the travellers were amused to see that the soap was impaled on an iron rod. But the place was comfortable and clean and, after a dinner of steak, eggs, *pommes frites* and beer, they went to bed, relieved to have found somewhere for the night.

Next morning, while the Gisbys and the Simpsons were having breakfast, three people came into the hotel: a woman with a little dog and, shortly afterwards, two *gendarmes*. They also seemed oddly antiquated. The woman wore a long dress and button-boots and the *gendarmes* were kitted out in gaiters, capes and high hats. Len Gisby remembers thinking that their uniforms were quite unlike those worn by the police they had passed on their way through France.

Below: Len Gisby's photographs of his French holiday hotel disappeared without trace. Detailed examination of the negatives revealed no blanks in the film and the frame numbers were consecutive.

The bill for the night came as a shock, but not for the usual reason. It was ridiculously low: a mere 19 francs (less than £2) for dinner, beer, bed and breakfast for all four. But the *patron* was insistent, and the Gisbys and Simpsons, hardly able to believe their luck, continued their journey to Spain.

A hotel offering so much for so little is a rare find indeed, and the couples naturally made for it on their way home. Once again they turned off the *autoroute* at the sign pointing to *Montélimar Nord* and followed the road past the Motel Ibis: exactly, they say, as they had done a fortnight before. The only difference was that this time the building seemed to have disappeared without trace. They drove round the area three times

before giving up in bewilderment. There was no sign of the house nor of the lay-by where they had parked on their way down. They had to make do with a hotel near Lyon which charged them 247 francs for their stay – realistic for 1979 but thirteen times as much as they had had to pay at the other quainter – and now mysterious – hostelry.

A few weeks later, when the couples' holiday snapshots came back from the processors, their puzzlement grew. Both Geoff and Len recalled taking photographs of their wives leaning out of the hotel bedroom windows just before breakfast, yet the negatives showed no trace of them. A careful examination revealed no blanks in the film and the serial numbers of the frames were consecutive.

The missing photographs made Cynthia Gisby wonder. Had they somehow travelled back into the past? Says Cynthia:

> A lot of people have said to me since about time-slips. I said, 'Well, I've never heard about time-slips,' and they said, 'Oh, there are such things, and we reckon that's what you've done.' But whether we did or not, I don't know. But the photographs worry me, and I think that alone convinces me that there is something not right.

In 1983 the Gisbys and Simpsons returned to France to mount a thorough search. By now, the local tourist board had been alerted and its representative, Philippe Despeysses, had combed the area. He reported that he had found a house roughly corresponding to the description given by the English couples. It was owned by a couple called M. and Mme Judges and, although it was not a proper hotel, they did take in travellers for bed, breakfast and an evening meal. Later, Despeysses drove there with a researcher who had interviewed the Gisbys and the

Simpsons. Afterwards the researcher wrote:

> We drove off in the direction they took and found ourselves on the road designated as RN 7. Philippe said nothing at first and simply waited to see if I could spot the house without his aid. I drew a blank though, so we reversed and he pulled into a large filling-station and pointed to a building opposite. The road we were in failed to match up to the description given by the Dover people. And if this *was* the house then where was the lay-by and stone wall that should have been facing it?
>
> These questions were soon answered by the owners of the filling-station. Their building was a newish structure (though they were uncertain exactly when it had been built), while the road had been considerably widened just two years ago.
>
> Our survey showed that the inside layout of the house differs from the descriptions provided by the couples. In the main this arises from a simple misplacement of the stone staircase. They said it was to the right of the 'bar-room', but in fact it is centrally placed between the two main downstairs rooms. And the 'bar-room' itself is simply a dining-room which has a large mahogany sideboard placed against the wall. This is often loaded up with bottles of wine and spirits and glasses, giving a bar-like appearance.
>
> Upstairs the two bedrooms are there, complete with high old-fashioned wooden beds and wooden-shuttered windows. The bathroom has now been refurbished but back in 1979 it was a semi-antique affair, equipped with a metal bar protruding from the wall to hold the soap.
>
> As for the absurdly small bill, Mme Judges said that they just don't like to be alone and they like helping people out, so they only charge something small – as a token.

So it was with some confidence that Philippe Despeysses took the Gisbys and the Simpsons to the house in 1983. At first they hesitated. 'It's very, very similar,' said Geoff Simpson. But a closer inspection and a chat with M. and Mme Judges convinced them that it was not the place they had stayed in four years before, and the couples returned home with the mystery as frustratingly unresolved as ever.

If the hotel in which the Gisbys and Simpsons spent the night in October 1979 turns out not to exist, then the case will go down as one of the most remarkable of all in the annals of psychical research. For most 'phantom scenery' is reported by people who have only seen it from a distance, yet the Gisbys and Simpsons, patently genuine and honest people, actually spent almost twelve hours inside the building and could later describe it in detail.

There are many loose ends still to tie up, however. An even more thorough search of the countryside around the *Montélimar Nord autoroute* exit may still locate the house. If it does, then the French 'phantom hotel' will turn out to be yet another case of what the experts call 'mislocation' – seeing a place, then failing to find it again and finally concluding that it existed only as a paranormal phenomenon. 'Mislocation' may also explain another intriguing case which has never been satisfactorily cleared up.

In the autumn of 1926 Miss Ruth Wynne, who had recently opened a 'dame school' at Rougham Rectory in Suffolk, was exploring the surrounding countryside with a fourteen-year-old pupil named Audrey Allington. They decided to walk across the fields and visit the church in the nearby hamlet of Bradfield St George. On the way, they came upon 'a high wall of greenish-yellow bricks'. In it was set a magnificent pair of wrought-iron gates.

> Behind the wall, [Miss Wynne reported] and towering above it was a cluster of tall trees. From the gates, a drive led away among these trees to what was evidently a large house. We

could just see a corner of the roof above a stucco front in which I remember noticing some windows of Georgian design.

Miss Wynne was puzzled. How curious not to have heard of 'one of the nearest large residences to our own, and it seemed odd that the occupants had not called.'

The following spring, the schoolteacher and her pupil went for the same walk. Said Miss Wynne:

We walked up through the farm-yard as before, and out on to the road, where, suddenly, we both stopped dead of one accord and gasped. 'Where's the wall?' we queried simultaneously. It was not there. The road was flanked by nothing but a ditch, and beyond the ditch lay a wilderness of tumbled earth, weeds, mounds, all overgrown with the trees we had seen on our first visit.

Had the house been demolished since their last walk? Apparently not, for they found 'a pond and other small pools amongst the mounds where the house had been visible. It was obvious that they had been there a long time.'

'We then returned home,' Miss Wynne recalled, 'half amused, half bothered, and yet convinced that we *had* seen that wall and house on the occasion of our first visit.'

Back in Rougham, the rector and his wife were equally puzzled, and villagers questioned denied all knowledge of the elusive house. Yet Miss Wynne was certain that she had seen it: 'I am convinced still that the house either once stood there, or else I shall meet it again somewhere else. I have often been past its site since, but I have never seen it again.'

In the past sixty years several psychical researchers have walked across those same Suffolk fields without finding any trace of the 'phantom house'. Yet the solution to this mystery may lie in Miss Wynne's original account. The first point to note is that Miss Wynne had only recently moved to Rougham. 'The district,' she wrote, 'was then entirely new to me.' Did her unfamiliarity with the local landscape cause her to make a mistake on her return visit to the area where she and her pupil had seen the mysterious house, leading them to confuse one location with another? How thorough was their search? Miss Wynne's parents, the first people questioned, were also recent arrivals in the area, and her own account mentions that she merely made 'various tentative inquiries of some villagers who lived near the site of our mystery, but they had never heard of a house existing at that spot, and obviously thought my question a foolish one, so I let the matter drop.' Finally both women were extremely vague about the building itself. Miss Wynne remembered seeing 'a corner of the roof above a stucco front' and a few 'windows of Georgian design', while Miss Allington says in her account, 'I can't remember the details of the house.' Had they really seen enough to recognize the building again? Though the case was obviously reported in good faith, it must remain very much unproven.

The Trianon Adventure

The most celebrated 'phantom scenery' mystery of all unfolded one August afternoon in 1901 when two English spinsters on holiday in France took a stroll through the gardens of the Palace of Versailles, home of the French kings in the seventeenth and eighteenth centuries, and walked, they believed, into the past. Both were utterly respectable, successful in their careers, and not, apparently, given to fantasy. Charlotte 'Annie' Moberly was principal of an Oxford college, Eleanor

Charlotte 'Annie' Moberly.   Eleanor Jourdain.

Jourdain the headmistress of a girls' school near London.

On the afternoon in question, 10 August 1901, the women were trying to reach the Petit Trianon, one of the most attractive of all the buildings dotted throughout the great park of Versailles. The map in their guidebook, however, was not clear, and they picked their way tentatively along the winding pathways and through the trees. According to their account, strange things happened as they walked. The people they came across seemed to be wearing eighteenth-century clothes. First, there was a woman shaking a white cloth out of the window of a building, then a couple of 'very dignified officials, dressed in long greyish-green coats with

small three-cornered hats'. Next, Miss Jourdain noticed a woman and a girl standing in the doorway of a nearby cottage. They too were dressed in the style of a bygone era: 'Both wore white kerchiefs tucked into the bodice, and the girl's dress, though she looked 13 or 14 only, was down to her ankles.' On her head she sported 'a close white cap'.

On they wandered to their most sinister encounter. On the steps of a kind of round summerhouse sat a man wearing 'a cloak and a large shady hat'. He 'slowly turned his face, which was marked by smallpox: his complexion was very dark. The expression was very evil and yet unseeing ...' Suddenly, they heard the sound of someone running, and a young man appeared as if from nowhere, shouting that they were going in the wrong direction. He wore a dark cloak 'wrapped across him like a scarf' and quaint buckle shoes.

At last they reached the Petit Trianon, where Miss Moberly, but curiously not Miss Jourdain, noticed a woman apparently sketching. Again, she seemed to be dressed in eighteenth-century style. Finally the women met a young man who directed them to the entrance. They both recalled that he had come out of a nearby building, slamming the door behind him.

Had the two English tourists glimpsed scenes from the past? When they compared notes, no other answer seemed possible; for what other explanation could there be for their encounters with people dressed in eighteenth-century clothes?

'Do you think that the Petit Trianon is haunted?' asked Miss Moberly.

'Yes I do,' replied Miss Jourdain.

Ten years later, their story was published, written pseudonymously and bolstered with research carried out at Versailles and in French archives. Despite its bland title, *An Adventure* was a sensation, for the women had concluded that during their walk in 1901 they had 'dropped in' on Versailles as it was in the 1780s, just before the French Revolution – the time of Marie-Antoinette and Louis XVI.

Do their claims bear scrutiny? Three-quarters of a century of controversy and analysis of *An Adventure* have thrown up arguments both for and against.

Supporters of Miss Moberly and Miss Jourdain point first to the findings of the research undertaken by the two women. These include their claim that the 'very dignified officials' they met early in their walk were wearing eighteenth-century royal livery, quite different to what was being worn at Versailles in 1901. The woman whom Miss Moberly had seen sitting near the Petit Trianon was identified as Marie-Antoinette herself from a contemporary portrait, and the journal of the queen's dressmaker provided the information that Marie-Antoinette had owned a dress exactly like the one the figure had been wearing in 1901. Much was made of the apparent correspondence of the landscape seen by Miss Moberly and Miss Jourdain, altered since the Revolution, to the Versailles of the eighteenth century.

Miss Jourdain provided another telling argument in favour of the time-slip claim. A few months after the first experience she returned to Versailles and again met people who seemed to belong more to the eighteenth than the twentieth century, including two curiously dressed men loading sticks into a cart. After consulting the Versailles wages book, Miss Jourdain concluded she had seen the 'cart with two horses (almost certainly requiring two men)' which had been hired for picking up wood in 1789. She also reported hearing strange music floating from afar which she later identified as 'the chief motifs of the light opera of the eighteenth century' – operas which, in many cases, had not been available since they were first played.

Further back-up came later from other people who claimed that they, too, had seen figures from the past at Versailles. Mr and Mrs Crooke and their son Stephen, who lived near the park in 1907 and 1908, said they saw several figures, including a 'sketching lady' like the one Miss Moberly had seen outside the Trianon, and a man in a three-cornered hat.

In 1928 Ann Lambert, a seventeen-year-old English schoolgirl, and her former

The Petit Trianon, Versailles, at the height of its
eighteenth-century glory.

Overleaf: The gardens of Versailles where Miss Jourdain and Miss Moberly had their 'adventure' in August 1901.

teacher, Miss Clare M. Burrow, came upon a strangely dressed gardener at Versailles. They had gone through a little gate and there he was, wearing a dingy brown corduroy jacket, knee breeches, black hose, buckle shoes and a hat turned up at the sides. He spoke in a curious way. To Miss Burrow, an accomplished linguist, it sounded perplexingly like an old, out-dated form of French, current 150 years before. An even stranger sight greeted them when they reached the Petit Trianon. A group of people – six or eight, Miss Lambert thought – stood on the lawn outside. Some were playing musical instruments; an elegant man and a beautiful woman were engaged in intimate conversation. All were arrayed in the most dazzling eighteenth-century costumes. With all the briskness of her calling, Miss Burrow ushered her fascinated pupil onward into the Trianon. 'It must be a pageant,' she said. Yet months later she confessed that she had made enquiries and had discovered that no pageant had been rehearsed or performed at Versailles that day. Even more puzzling was the revelation that the gate through which they had passed before meeting the gardener had apparently been sealed up for more than 100 years.

At least one Frenchman claims to have seen the ghosts of Versailles. Robert Philippe, an art teacher and cabinet maker, was walking in the park with his parents one June day in the 1930s, when he found himself obliged by a sudden call of nature to go behind a tree. There, to his embarrassment, he felt a presence. A mysterious woman had appeared by his side, as if from nowhere. Quite unabashed, she engaged him in conversation. Did she live in Paris? asked the nonplussed M. Philippe. No, at the Trianon. 'But I thought the Trianon was uninhabited.'

'Yes,' came the reply, 'but not for me.' The young man looked away for a moment and relit a cigarette. When he looked up, the woman had gone. His parents, who had been waiting nearby, had seen no one and had imagined that, for some reason, their son had been talking to himself behind the tree.

Nevertheless, the sceptics have marshalled a formidable case against the claims of the two 'adventurers'. They have pointed out that the descriptions of the people encountered are so vague that it is, for example, impossible to decide whether they were wearing authentic eighteenth-century dress or clothes that were merely rustic or somewhat old-fashioned. Why, they ask, did the two women not discuss their experience immediately after the walk, over their tea at the Hôtel des Réservoirs – instead of waiting a week to compare notes? Why do their accounts of the 'adventure', written at various times before the book was published, differ markedly? In particular, why do telling details, missing from the earliest versions, suddenly appear in later ones?

Perhaps most crucial of all is the women's reluctance to look for, and accept, a natural explanation for the events of that summer afternoon. They were, after all, in unfamiliar surroundings and had lost their way in a maze of pathways and thickets; the weather was sultry and there was an oppressive, brooding atmosphere – the kind that often precedes a thunderstorm. In such circumstances imagination can work overtime, and even the most respectable of academic ladies may be forgiven for indulging in romantic reverie, especially since, as one critic has put it,

> there are few places in the world in which it is easier to imagine ghosts than the vast palace of Versailles. The echoing halls of the great

Comte Robert de Montesquiou-Fezenzac dressed in
eighteenth-century costume for a *tableau vivant* at
Versailles.

who settled for a down-to-earth explanation.
She discovered from a book published in the
1960s that a rakish aristocrat called Comte
Robert de Montesquiou-Fezenzac had been
obsessed with the fashions of the eighteenth
century and often wore clothes of the period.
Moreover, he frequented the gardens of
Versailles and organized *tableaux vivants* or
pageants in which he and his cronies wore
eighteenth-century costume. Dame Joan
concluded that Miss Moberly and Miss
Jourdain had stumbled upon one of the
count's rehearsals and that all the people
they had met in the gardens had been acting.

Miss Moberly is known to have mistaken
a real person for a ghost on at least one
occasion. Two years after *An Adventure* was
published she visited the Louvre in Paris,
where she noticed an extraordinary man. He
had 'a small golden coronal on his head, and
wore a loose toga-like dress of some light
colour'. After much research, she decided
that she had seen the ghost of the Roman
Emperor Constantine, who had marched in
procession down the road over which the
Louvre was later built. But this exotic little
scenario was demolished in the 1960s when
a Sunday newspaper revealed that there had
been an artist living in Paris at the time of
the 'vision' who had gone about dressed as a
Roman, complete with gold crown, in protest
at the ugliness of current fashions.

In a letter to *The Times* it was suggested
that Miss Moberly had also jumped to the
wrong conclusion in her identification of the
'sketching lady':

At the end of a talk on *An Adventure* which I
gave . . . to the Académie de Versailles, [wrote
T. G. S. Combe in 1965] a member of my audience informed me that when she was a child
there lived in her district at Versailles a lady
who, in the summer, used to dress up as Marie-

château, the labyrinthine walks of the main
park with their stone benches and frozen statu-
ary, the haunted gardens of the Petit Trianon
– all are alike murmurous with the footfalls of
history.

Dame Joan Evans, an Oxford art historian
and friend and literary executor of the two
authors of *An Adventure*, was one of those

Antoinette and go and sit in the garden of the Petit Trianon. That Miss Moberly saw this lady seems at least more likely than that she could have seen Marie-Antoinette herself.

Did the two women perhaps share a sort of waking dream? A close reading of *An Adventure* suggests they did, for they repeatedly refer to an eerie, unreal atmosphere that seemed to pervade the park: 'Everything suddenly looked unnatural, therefore unpleasant; even the trees behind the building seemed to have become flat and lifeless, *like a wood worked in tapestry* [their italics]. There were no effects of light and shade, and no wind stirred the trees. It was all intensely still.' They claimed to have known little about Versailles before their visit, yet what they actually saw demanded no more than the ability to distinguish outmoded clothes from the fashions of 1901. Moreover, Miss Jourdain had taught French history and they had a guidebook with them. Assuming that they did see people on their walk, could they simply have embroidered the facts, vested them with historical significance, dreamt a little? Were there other sources for their 'scenario'? For example, a bestselling novel about time travel called *Lumen*, in which the hero sees the French Revolution happening seventy years after the actual events, had been published in England as recently as 1897, and a story about Marie-Antoinette from *Pearson's Magazine* (published in 1893) has many phrases curiously similar to those used by the two ladies to describe their experience.

Was *An Adventure* a fantasy shared by two avowed believers in psychical phenomena which finally got out of hand, or did Miss Moberly and Miss Jourdain really take a stroll into the past on that August afternoon in 1901? Both are now long dead and we shall never know the answer. The trail, frustratingly, has now gone cold.

Yet cases of phantom scenery continue to surface.

Scene Changes

One evening in April 1955 Mrs Susannah Stone, who lives near Tain in Ross and Cromarty in the north of Scotland, was driving a friend home after dinner. It was about 9.30, and although the sun had set it was still light. Just outside the town of Alness, Mrs Stone says that she and her companion spotted a house on fire:

> It was a perfectly ordinary house, with a long narrow door in the middle and long windows – quite big, like a farmhouse. It was blazing. Flames were curling out of the windows. I said, 'My God, what a fire! Poor things!'
>
> We were about a quarter of a mile away and my friend said, 'Let's go down and have a closer look.' It never occurred to me that I'd never seen a house there before.
>
> We went nearer and it wasn't there.

Mystified, Mrs Stone drove on, but after dropping her friend she returned to the site of the 'fire'. By now, it was much later: a punctured tyre had delayed her. This time, she walked up the road. She found nothing. 'No fire, no glow, no ashes, no people, nothing,' she says. And the next day, when she checked, she discovered that the fire brigade *had* been called out – but to a blaze in a couple of haystacks thirty miles from Mrs Stone's mysterious sighting, and in the opposite direction. As far as she can discover, no house of any kind has ever stood on the spot. The experience remains unexplained. It was, says Susannah Stone, 'very creepy'.

In the late 1940s the Reverend Alfred Byles was Vicar of Yealmpton, South Devon. One Saturday afternoon, while his wife was

Below: The Rev. Alfred Byles is still mystified by the
hole which appeared and then vanished in his
country churchyard.

arranging the altar flowers, he noticed something strange in the churchyard. He wrote
later:

> In the middle of the path I saw a hole, of
> irregular shape, about a yard in width. I
> thought it was subsidence, and went into the
> church and told my wife about it. Coming out
> shortly afterwards, I found that the hole was
> very much larger, and asked my wife to come
> out and see it. We both looked into it, and I
> suggested lowering myself into it. However, it
> was of uncertain depth, and when I threw in a
> stone it bumped against stonework, which we
> could see and which looked like part of a wall.
>
> My main concern was to prevent an accident

to anyone using the path. I therefore went away
to get some planks to cover the hole, which
measured about three yards across. In the village street I met Mr Knight, the local builder
and undertaker, and asked him to come and
see the hole. On arrival there was no sign of a
hole. The path and the grass verges were
exactly as before, with no sign of disturbance.
Mr Knight seemed rather less puzzled than I
expected, and said, 'That's all right, sir,' or
words to that effect. He never mentioned the
incident again.

Mr Byles, on the other hand, was far less
phlegmatic. He was mystified, and remained
so more than thirty years later. 'We both of

us saw the original hole,' he said, 'and we've never found any adequate explanation.'

Explanations for 'phantom scenery' are indeed hard to establish: optical illusion, hallucination and 'mislocation' are some of the weapons in the sceptics' armoury, while other investigators have tried to explain the phenomenon in terms of 'retrocognition', arguing that, for reasons not yet understood, a few rare individuals may briefly be allowed to unlatch a door to the past and peer inside. There are few ideas more beguiling. Lucille Iremonger, author of the definitive work on the 'Trianon adventure', expressed its appeal perfectly:

> It is the question that has always haunted man - the question that informs the myths and legends of the ancient world, in which Orpheus visits the underworld and the Sibyl foretells the future; the question whether a human mind can experience happenings outside the narrow groove in which it normally runs . . . whether, in fact, you or I could at any moment step back into the past, or – and this follows – out into the future.
>
> That question has not yet been answered with a decisive yes or no.

Arthur C. Clarke comments:

Since 1966 the Science Fiction Writers of America have issued an annual Nebula Award for the year's best fiction in all categories. The short story prize for that year went to Richard McKenna's 'The Secret Place'.

Unfortunately, McKenna had died two years before at the age of fifty-one having published only six short stories in his lifetime. Like Alex ('Roots') Haley, he was a self-made writer who had risen from the ranks in the US Navy by sheer determination. They both deserved success, and they both achieved it – for McKenna's first and only novel, *The Sand Pebbles* (1962), was a bestseller and later an excellent film, starring Steve McQueen and featuring a promising young actor named Dickie Attenborough.

'The Secret Place' is one of those very few stories which quite literally make the hair stand up on the back of my neck (even *thinking about* it is doing so right now). It concerns a young girl in the Oregon desert who has visions of a time when the landscape was very different:

> 'That's where all the dogs are,' she said.
> 'Dogs?'
> I looked around at the scrubby sagebush and thin soil and ugly black rock and back at Helen. Something was wrong.
> 'Big, stupid dogs that go in herds and eat grass,' she said. She kept turning and gazing. 'Big cats chase the dogs and eat them. The dogs scream and scream. Can't you hear them?'

Well, some of the visions described in this chapter also appear to go back in time – though not quite as far as the Early Miocene, approximately twenty-five million years ago. Even if, like McKenna's story, they are pure fiction, they certainly demonstrate the power of the human imagination.

And there may be more to it than that. Do we yet know all the ways in which records of the past have been preserved? Let me quote from the most famous science fiction writer of all:

> A day may come when these recovered memories may grow as vivid as if we in our own persons had been there and shared the thrill and fear of those primordial days; a day may come when the great beasts of the past will leap to life again in our imaginations, when we shall walk again in vanished scenes, stretch painted limbs we thought were dust, and feel again the sunshine of a million years ago (H. G. Wells, *The Grisly Folk*).

Frances and the dancing fairies (Photograph A).

7.

Fairies, Phantoms, Fantastic Photographs

The Cottingley Fairies

On 17 July 1972 a most mysterious lot went under the hammer at Sotheby's salerooms in Bond Street, London. At first glance, there was nothing particularly impressive about its contents. There were a couple of old cameras, five old photographs, and a letter from Sir Arthur Conan Doyle, creator of Sherlock Holmes, to a girl from a country village in the north of England. Yet, although the sale contained other, far more obviously desirable lots (five previously unknown letters by the American poet Walt Whitman, original manuscripts by the Victorian artist and poet William Morris, and even a painting by D. H. Lawrence, author of *Lady Chatterley's Lover*), it was this strange and rather scruffy collection of objects which stole the limelight. For on offer that Monday morning was a dossier on a case which had first intrigued, then baffled and finally frustrated psychical researchers for more than half a century: the strange tale of the Cottingley fairies.

The five photographs lay at the heart of the mystery, for they purported to show real fairies dancing beside a stream at Cottingley in Yorkshire. The pictures were taken between 1917 and 1920 by two young girls. Did they really prove that fairies exist?

At least one influential figure believed they did. By 1920, Sir Arthur Conan Doyle was one of the most celebrated literary figures in the world, thanks to his Sherlock Holmes novels and stories; and his support for the Boer War and other causes of the age had earned him the respect of the British public. So when the 1920 Christmas number of the monthly *Strand Magazine* appeared, emblazoned with the headline, FAIRIES PHOTOGRAPHED. AN EPOCH-MAKING EVENT DESCRIBED BY A. CONAN DOYLE, there was a sensation. With the article, the great man published two of the photographs (the others followed later in the March 1921 edition) and asserted in terms which, despite some slight show of scepticism, did not really invite much in the way of contradiction, 'Should the incidents here narrated, and the photographs attached, hold their own against the criticism which they will excite, it is no exaggeration to say that they will mark an epoch in human thought.'

The story Conan Doyle had to tell did indeed appear remarkable. In the summer of 1917 a little girl of ten called Frances Griffiths was staying with her cousin, Elsie Wright, then aged fifteen. They used to while away the days in a wild patch of countryside just below Elsie's garden, known as Cottingley Glen. A stream ran through the middle and on its mossy banks, the girls asserted, they regularly saw fairies. When the grown-ups did not seem to believe them, Elsie and Frances appeared surprised, and when scepticism gave way to teasing, the girls were outraged. They would, they announced, provide proof.

Opposite: Elsie and the gnome (Photograph B).

Elsie's father, Arthur Wright, was an amateur photographer, keen enough to have established his own darkroom in the scullery cupboard. Neither girl had ever taken a photograph before, but Elsie persuaded her father to lend her his camera, a popular box-type called a Midg, which he had bought from his uncle for 7s. 6d. The Midg took photographs on a series of individual plates, and Arthur loaded just one of them into the camera before the girls set off for their 'rendezvous' with the Cottingley fairies. Before long they were back, excited and eager for the photograph to be developed. Arthur Wright took the plate into the darkroom. Elsie, who had acted as photographer, went too. Under the safelight, the image on the plate began to look very odd indeed. Arthur could make out Frances's face and her right arm and shoulder, but what were those weird white blobs that surrounded her?

Next day, after the picture had been laboriously printed, came the answer. It showed Frances looking thoughtful, her chin leaning on her right hand. In the foreground, the grasses and wild flowers of Cottingley Glen provided a leafy frame, while the background was indistinct. But, astonishingly, the white blobs which had puzzled Arthur Wright turned out to be four captivating fairies, dressed in swirling gowns. One was playing a musical instrument, while the others, arms upraised and legs elegantly pointed, danced joyfully to the music. Every detail came out sharply: the veins of their wings, their silken tresses, the fingers of the fairies' tiny hands. Arthur Wright, though by all accounts impressed by the quality of his daughter's first attempt at photography, was apparently amused but unconvinced. Despite the 'evidence' so speedily furnished, tales of fairies at the bottom of the garden continued to be greeted with raised eyebrows by the grown-ups.

A few weeks later, the girls again borrowed the camera. This time it was Frances's turn to be the photographer. The picture she took was even more remarkable than the first, for it apparently showed Elsie greeting a grotesque little gnome on a bank at the top of the glen. The creature was conventionally dressed, for a gnome, in black tights; he also wore a jersey through which his wings poked, and on his head was a little pointed cap. He certainly seemed alive, as though he had just rushed out of the long grass to greet his human friend. But once again, Arthur Wright was apparently more impressed by the children's skill as photographers than by their claim to have proved the existence of fairies.

And there the matter might have rested if Elsie's mother, Polly Wright, had not gone to a lecture in nearby Bradford, where she happened to mention that she had a couple of photographs of fairies at home. The lecturer asked to see them and, when they arrived, she passed them on to a friend in London, Edward L. Gardner, a confirmed believer in the existence of fairies. Gardner, in his turn, asked to see the original negatives; when they reached him, he bicycled from his home in Harlesden to consult an expert photographer, Mr H. Snelling, who pronounced the pictures genuine and furnished Gardner with a letter guaranteeing their authenticity:

> These two negatives are entirely genuine un-faked photographs of single exposure, open-air work, [they] show movement in the fairy figures, and there is no trace whatever of studio work involving card or paper models, dark backgrounds, painted figures etc. In my opinion, they are both straight untouched pictures.

Frances and the leaping fairy (Photograph C).

Elsie and the flower fairy (Photograph D).

The 'fairy bower' (Photograph E).

Below: Fairies frolic over the Alhambra Theatre, Bradford. Yorkshire photographer Dot Inman produced this picture to show that the Cottingley photographs could have been faked.

Soon, Conan Doyle had become involved, and after Gardner had visited the Wrights in Yorkshire and pronounced himself satisfied that the pictures had not been faked, the famous author wrote his article for the *Strand Magazine.*

As Conan Doyle had predicted before the magazine was published, his revelations did indeed stimulate controversy. While he and Gardner defended the girls against any imputation that they had perpetrated a hoax upon their trusting elders, the sceptics set about trying to discover how the photographs could have been faked.

Meanwhile Frances and Elsie had come up with three more remarkable pictures, this time taken with cameras of their own which Gardner had given them. These were published in the *Strand Magazine* in March 1921. The first showed Frances apparently staring at a leaping fairy. Elsie featured in the next one alongside a fairy who was offering her a posy of flowers. Finally, there was the strangest photograph of all, which became known as the 'fairy bower'. Gardner offered this interpretation of it:

> This is especially remarkable as it contains a feature quite unknown to the girls. The sheath or cocoon appearing in the middle of the grasses had not been seen by them before, and they had no idea what it was. Fairy observers of Scotland and the New Forest, however, were familiar with it and described it as a magnetic bath . . .

In the face of Conan Doyle's repeated assertions that the pictures were genuine, and his contention that two young girls would not have been capable of faking such remarkable photographs, the sceptics made little headway. Some, like Miss Dot Inman, a Yorkshire photographer, produced 'fairy photographs' of their own to demonstrate that fraud was possible: her most charming effort showed the little creatures soaring above the domes of Bradford's Alhambra Theatre. Others, assuming that the girls had modelled their fairies upon those in a painting or drawing, searched for the source of their inspiration: an advertisement for Price's nightlights was deemed the most likely candidate. The public, however, was amused, and while Gardner and Conan Doyle toured the world lecturing about the Cottingley fairies, the girls themselves kept silent.

As the years passed, the story surfaced from time to time. In 1971 Elsie appeared on a BBC news magazine programme, *Nationwide*. Four years later, she and Frances were interviewed in *Woman* magazine, and in 1977 they revisited Cottingley for a Yorkshire Television film. Despite persistent

Below: Claude A. Shepperson's vignette from *Princess Mary's Gift Book*. For the first Cottingley photograph, Elsie copied the fairies, added wings and rearranged them.

questioning from the reporters, they stuck to their story.

The revival of interest in the case attracted the attention of a new generation of sceptics. In 1973 Professor Stuart Sanderson discussed the Cottingley mystery in his Presidential Address to the Folklore Society. Having begun his speech by declaring his scepticism about the genuineness of the photographs, he went on to raise a list of pertinent questions. Why, for example, had the girls been unable to photograph fairies when a third party was present? He also pointed out that Elsie might, after all, have been able to produce fakes, for not only was

she a talented artist and had been known to paint fairies, but she had also worked in a photographer's studio.

Four years later, Fred Gettings, a researcher well-versed both in art and the paranormal, came across an important clue. He was leafing through a copy of *Princess Mary's Gift Book*, a compilation of stories, pictures and poems sold in aid of charity and a bestseller in 1915, two years before the Cottingley fairy photographs were taken. One contribution was a poem by Alfred Noyes called 'A Spell for a Fairy', illustrated by Claude A. Shepperson. The final vignette on page 104 of the *Gift Book* stopped Gettings

in his tracks. He recognized it as

> without doubt, the original picture from which the fairies of the first Cottingley picture were constructed. The remarkable thing is that the girl who copied this (presumably Elsie, as she was the older and more artistically talented of the two) actually made no significant change to the individual figures of the fairies in the Shepperson drawing – they merely appear in the photograph in a different order. Elsie's drawing is clumsier, and she added butterfly wings to the figures.

At least one other person might have been expected to have reached the same conclusion more than fifty years earlier, for on page 23 of the *Gift Book* begins a story called 'Bimbashi Joyce'. Its author? None other than Sir Arthur Conan Doyle!

In 1980 arch-sceptic James 'the Amazing' Randi devoted a chapter of his book, *Flim-Flam*, to the debunking of the photographs. Randi revealed that the latest 'computer enhancement' techniques, designed to bring out the smallest details of satellite photographs, had 'put a very large nail of doubt in the already well-sealed coffin of the Cottingley Fairies'. The computer had been asked whether the fairy figures were three-dimensional. No, they weren't, it replied. The conclusion was obvious: the fairies were cardboard cut-outs. In a second test, the computer searched for threads or supports which could have been used to prop up the figures. It found something suspiciously like a thread in the fourth picture, although Randi was less convinced by this than by the earlier finding. He concluded:

> The Cottingley fairies were simple fakes made by two little girls as a prank, in the beginning. Only when supposedly wiser persons discovered them were they elevated to the status of miracles, and the girls were caught up in an

ever-escalating situation that they wanted out of but could not escape.

For the sceptics, the case of the Cottingley fairies was frustrating. They were certain the pictures were faked, yet they had no absolute proof and, as the years passed, there seemed little prospect of obtaining any. 'Quite how they were faked,' mused Stuart Sanderson in his 1973 address to the Folklore Society, 'we shall probably never know.'

Yet we now do know, and indeed would have done so a few months before Sanderson's speech if Sotheby's experts had looked with greater understanding at a letter which Elsie had sent with her Cottingley memorabilia for sale in 1972. It contained a detailed explanation by Elsie of how the two girls had hoaxed the world. But because the letter was obviously recently written and the sale was of antique literary documents only, the experts returned it to Elsie; and unwittingly delayed the final solution of the mystery for another decade.

The Cottingley Mystery solved

The breakthrough came when two investigators, independently of each other, took a fresh look at the case in the 1980s. One was Geoffrey Crawley, editor of the prestigious *British Journal of Photography*; the other was Joe Cooper, a sociologist who had long been interested in the paranormal.

Crawley's investigation, which began its serialization in the *BJP* on Christmas Eve 1982, was exhaustive and fascinating but also quite technical – exactly what might be expected of a top photographic expert. One of Crawley's first decisions was to examine not only the five pictures but also the cameras used by the girls. Fortunately, the Midg camera that Elsie had borrowed from her father was still in existence: it had been one of the mementoes she had sent for sale at Sotheby's in 1972. Crawley borrowed it, took a few test photographs, and noticed something that all the other investigators had apparently missed. The lens of the Midg camera could not possibly have provided a photograph of the depth and clarity of the first published fairy picture. The implication was clear: the picture of Frances and the dancing fairies (Crawley labelled it Photograph A), which had been accepted for more than sixty years as the original, had been heavily retouched and then rephotographed. The same went for Photograph B (Elsie and the gnome).

Then Crawley had the kind of luck that comes to the diligent researcher. A different version of Photograph A turned up in Cottingley itself. It was far less sharp than the one originally published: Frances's face and hair have a washed-out look, the fairies are little more than white blobs, and the foliage in the foreground is indistinct. It was exactly the type of photograph Crawley would have expected from a novice like Elsie using an unsophisticated camera like a Midg.

Crawley next turned to Photograph B. Although he was unable to trace an authentic first print of it, a close examination of what had always been held to be the original negative, kept in the Brotherton Library at Leeds University, revealed a telling detail. A photograph taken with a Midg camera always showed certain marks, yet there were none on the 'original'. The sheath in which each plate was held would also have imprinted its shape on to the image, yet there was no trace of it on Photograph B. Another clue was that the colour of the 'original' prints was wrong. Surviving family photographs show that Arthur Wright, like most amateur photographers of his day, used day-light printing paper. He always fixed the negative to the paper and left it out in the sun to develop. The resulting prints were sepia-coloured. But the published fairy pictures were all a rich blue-black which could only have been achieved in a darkroom.

By looking at the negatives of the improved photographs, Crawley was even able to tell how the pictures had been retouched. But who had been responsible? The most likely candidate was Edward Gardner's friend Mr Snelling, who had guaranteed the authenticity of the photographs in the first place. Snelling was an acknowledged expert in the techniques of improving photographs – an art more widely practised in the first two decades of this century than it is today.

While Crawley's revelations did not prove that the girls had faked the original photographs, they did increase his suspicions about their authenticity, and his examination of the last three pictures reinforced his doubts. He concluded that each of them was a superimposition, difficult to achieve with a Midg but easy with the new Cameo cameras the girls had been given. In phototgraphs C and D, Crawley suggested, a cut-out fairy was first photographed indoors; the plate was then re-exposed down in Cottingley Glen. One clue supporting this theory is that in the finished photographs neither of the girls manages to look directly at the fairy. The final picture, Crawley believed, was an accidental double-exposure. He agreed with another photographic expert, Brian Coe, who suggested that the girls had tried to take two separate photographs of some cut-out figures in the grass, but had managed to mix up the plates so that both images appeared on the same one.

Meanwhile Joe Cooper had been to see Elsie and Frances. Both were old ladies, and

The original version of the first Cottingley picture, before it was retouched and rephotographed.

Frances, then seventy-five, finally broke her long silence. She admitted that the first four fairy photographs were fakes, and that she had always felt guilty about the first one, in particular. 'My heart always sinks when I look at it,' she said. 'When I think of how it's gone all round the world – I don't see how people could believe they're real fairies. I could see the backs of them and the hatpins when the photo was being taken.' She confirmed that the fairy figures had indeed been cut-outs. Elsie had drawn them, and the dancing figures in the first photograph had been copied from *Princess Mary's Gift Book*, as Fred Gettings had deduced. But there had been nothing fake about the fifth photograph, she claimed. It had been of the real

fairies that lived in the glen. According to Cooper, 'Elsie, on the other hand, insists that all five photographs are of cut-outs.'

Elsie then wrote to Geoffrey Crawley, who had sent her some sections of his series in advance. Her letter was, he realized, 'the authentic document confirming that the so-styled "Cottingley fairy photographs" taken in 1917 and 1920 were not of paranormal phenomena'.

Dear Mr Crawley [the letter began],
Thank you for your letter revealing so much depth and understanding of the pickle Frances and I got ourselves into on that day back in 1916 [*sic*] when our practical joke fell flat on its face, when no one would believe we had got pictures of real fairies. Just imagine (if they

Elsie Wright and one of the fairy photographs which baffled investigators for more than seventy years.

had) the joke would have ended there and then, when we would have told all, when I was 15 years old, and Frances was 8 [sic] years old.

Over the months that followed, the cousins gradually owned up to a prank which had started innocently but had soon got out of hand. This is the story that emerged.

In the summer of 1917, when the two girls used to play by Cottingley beck, Frances would talk of seeing fairies along its leafy banks. All too often the younger girl fell into the water and returned home to the Wrights' house with soaking wet shoes, stockings and knickers. One night, Frances recalled, matters came to a head. Her mother was furious, not simply because Frances had wet clothes but because neither she nor Elsie's mother could understand why the girls were so keen on playing by the beck.

She said that she and Aunt Polly had been up the beck and they'd found nothing. They couldn't see anything at all. It was just trees and water and ferns and what-have-you. You could have that anywhere. You didn't have to go right up the beck to see that. I don't know why, but I'd had enough, and I blurted out 'I go up to see the fairies'. At that time Uncle Arthur had come in and Elsie had come in, and Aunt Polly was there. They all stood round looking at me and my mother got annoyed and she said "Well that beats the lot! You've started telling lies on top of being naughty all the time and getting wet and ruining all your good shoes.' And then she stopped and she turned round and said to Elsie, 'Have you seen these fairies?' And Elsie, she stuck up for me, and she said 'Yes.'

Inevitably, the grown-ups began to tease the girls about their fairy friends. Their gentle sarcasm maddened Elsie, the protective elder cousin. She resolved to do something to stop it. Sixty-seven years later, Frances recalled how Elsie revealed her plan:

> One night, as we were getting ready for bed, she said, 'I've been thinking kid (she was a real cinema-goer, was Elsie), what about if I draw some fairies and cut them out in cardboard and we'll stick them up in the grass and see if Dad will lend us the camera and we'll take a photograph. If they see them they'll *have* to believe. It'll stop all this joking.'

So the girls talked a reluctant Arthur Wright into lending them the Midg camera, after promising not to drop it into the water, and set off up Cottingley Glen.

> Elsie had her fairies down her bosom [Frances remembered]. We went up the beck and wandered round and decided on this little bank beside the beck because I could get behind it and there were toadstools growing there and it was pretty and in the sunlight. She stuck the fairies in artistic places, one on top of a toadstool standing on one toe, which she was very proud of, and took the photograph.

That first picture, and the second one of the gnome, certainly stopped the teasing, but since the grown-ups did not believe the fairies were real, the girls never had the chance to explain how they faked the photographs. Then Conan Doyle and Edward Gardner pronounced them to be genuine. Why didn't the girls confess the truth?

> It was all very embarrassing [Elsie recalled]. We were two village kids with a brilliant man like Conan Doyle. Well, we could only keep quiet. We'd have hurt him terribly to do a thing

like that. It would have been like two kids taking the mickey out of him. And Frances didn't want me to tell because the schoolkids were giving her an awful time at school and, she says, it'll just bring it on worse.

Frances, in her turn, had promised Elsie never to reveal their secret.

> Elsie had said to me after the first one, 'Now look, you don't tell anybody about this. Promise?' And I promised. And I got this silly idea that a promise was a promise and I couldn't break it. Later on I didn't want to, I just wanted to forget it. I didn't want anybody to know. I thought if I don't say anything it'll die a natural death, but it didn't. It was as simple as that.

Almost three-quarters of a century after the two young cousins took that first famous photograph, the story was still making headlines. When Frances died in July 1986 she still maintained to the end that although the first four photographs had been fakes, the fifth really had captured the hidden fairy kingdom she had found as a child in Cottingley Glen. When the obituary-writers questioned Elsie, she took the opportunity once again to set the record straight about the long-running 'fairytale'. 'The joke,' she said, 'was to last two hours, and it has lasted seventy years.'

The Spirit Photographers

The fashion for spiritualism was less than fifteen years old – the Fox sisters had begun it in 1848 – when a few enterprising photographers announced that, for a suitable fee, they could capture the images of dead people on photographic plates. Grieving parents, widows and widowers queued up to pose and were rewarded by the discovery of a strange, if often blurred figure hovering beside them on the developed picture, which many of them unhesitatingly declared to be

Below: The 'spirit extra' of assassinated American
President Abraham Lincoln appeared on William
Mumler's photograph of his widow.

a consoling likeness of their departed loved-ones.

One of the first of the spirit photographers was an American called William Mumler, who set up shop in Boston, Massachusetts, in the 1860s. He had been plying his weird trade for only a few months, however, when he was caught out by several of his more sceptical sitters and run out of town. Apparently some of the 'spirits' – or 'extras', as they were known – bore more than a passing likeness to living people. Yet he was soon in business again, and a few years later could

boast a list of famous clients, including Mrs Lincoln, wife of the assassinated President. Mrs Lincoln is said to have visited Mumler under an assumed name and with her face heavily veiled, but when a figure looking very much like the recently departed Abe appeared on the finished portrait, the First Widow apparently broke down and confessed her true identity. Mumler's career took another dive in 1869 when he was put on trial for fraud. The Mayor of New York, suspecting Mumler of trickery, ordered one of his men, Marshal J. H. Tooker, to investigate. Tooker assumed a false name and went to have his picture taken. When a 'spirit' appeared on the processed plate, Mumler assured the marshal that it was the image of his dead father-in-law. Tooker, however, saw no resemblance whatsoever, and promptly arrested Mumler. But the evidence produced at the trial at Tombs Police Court, New York, was flimsy, and although Justice Dowling indicated that he believed 'trick and deception had been practised by the prisoner', he had to conclude that there was no case to answer.

Other 'spirit photographers' flourished on both sides of the Atlantic, relying for their lucrative pickings upon a combination of public ignorance of the new-fangled art of photography and the desperate desire of the bereaved to contact their dead loved-ones. They, too, were frequently caught cheating. For example, Jean Buguet, French high society's favourite 'spirit photographer', was put on trial in 1875, and the court was told that many of the 'extras' in his pictures had been cardboard heads and elegantly draped dummies, spirited on to the plate by double-exposure.

The sceptics were hard-pressed to keep up with all the techniques used by fraudulent 'spirit photographers' – at least 200 methods have been identified. Most used double-exposures of one kind or another. In the shadows of the studio or the gloom of the darkroom it was easy to switch plates provided by the sitter for a set with ghostly images already imprinted upon them. An American investigator, Joseph H. Kraus, discovered some even more elaborate tricks. One medium, Madame Eva, amazed her sitters by apparently producing a bright halo across her chest when she was photographed. According to Kraus, however, she had merely dipped the piece of gauze she wore to conceal her cleavage in luminous paint which glowed under the photographer's lights. Others, using sleight-of-hand, slipped prepared transparencies into the lens or concealed doctored plates in secret compartments in their camera cases – a method Kraus's fellow-sceptic, the conjuror Joseph Dunninger, was fond of demonstrating. Hidden slide projectors, chemicals secretly dripped through the ceiling on to developing trays, walls painted with fluorescent paints invisible to the naked eye but which could be illuminated for the camera with ultra-violet lights, even radium plates and X-ray machines were all used by the unscrupulous tricksters.

So many 'spirit photos' were taken at the height of the craze that the methods of some of the charlatans have only recently been exposed. One of the most colourful and successful of the British 'psychographers' was Dr T. d'Aute Hooper, a one-legged faith-healer and medium from Birmingham – a man, according to his supporters, who was 'far above trickery and any sordid dealing'. One day, one of Hooper's patients, who happened to be staying with him, returned from a walk and said, 'Doctor, I feel so queer, I feel as if there is someone with me; will you get your camera and take a snap-shot at me?' Hooper wrote:

> I got the camera and before I exposed the plate I told him I saw a beautiful child with him. I put a dark table-cloth over the door in the drawing-room to form a back-ground and then exposed the plate. The gentleman himself took the plate to the dark room and developed it; and there appeared the beautiful spirit form of a little girl with a bouquet of flowers in one hand and a roll of paper in the other. The exclamation of the gentleman was 'Good heavens! It's my daughter, who died thirty years ago.'

Dr Hooper, who obviously regarded this picture as a first-class advertisement for his powers, kept a copy, and it was published in 1919. Over the next sixty years it reappeared

'For You' by Charles T. Garland: the painting Dr Hooper incorporated into the 'spirit photograph' to dupe his patient.

Opposite: The Raynham Hall 'ghost'.

frequently in books and articles, and was often cited as proof that spirits could be photographed. In the 1980s, however, one of the periodic flurries of interest in psychic photography coincided with the reprinting (for greetings cards and a poster) of a picture called 'For You' by Charles T. Garland. Painted in 1879, it had been used to advertise Pears soap around the turn of the century. When they saw the reproductions in the shops, several researchers realized that the little girl in Garland's picture was identical to the 'spirit' which had appeared in Hooper's photograph. Wrote one: 'The clairvoyant photograph is, I think, just a clever double-exposure. Another ghost "laid" I fear.'

So how was it that Hooper's patient recognized the girl in the picture as his dead daughter? Perhaps, in his grief, he had been clutching at straws, a victim of understandable self-delusion. As one expert on psychic photographs wrote scathingly in 1875: 'Some people would recognize anything. A broom and a sheet are quite enough to make up a grandmother for some wild enthusiasts who . . . see what they wish to see.' It was a wish that the 'spirit photographers' exploited to the full.

'Ghost' Photographs

Frances and Elsie, and 'spirit photographers' like Mumler and Dr Hooper, claimed to be able to produce psychic pictures on demand, but some of the weirdest images of all have simply turned up on photographs taken by people who later claim to have seen nothing extraordinary through their viewfinder at the time of pressing the button. Many can simply be explained away as double-exposures. One example is the famous 'Raynham Hall ghost'. The picture was taken in September 1936 by a fashionable London photographer who claimed to have seen 'an ethereal, veiled form coming slowly down the stairs' of the great house. The resulting picture was indeed eerie, yet at least one modern expert is unconvinced, pointing to the number of double images that can be made out in it. For example, there is a pale line above each stair-tread, indicating that one picture has been imprecisely superimposed over the other; a patch of reflected light at the top of the right-hand bannister appears twice.

Other 'ghost' photographs have proved more difficult to explain, and in 1984 some of the most puzzling examples were analyzed by two experts, Dr Steve Gull and his col-

This mysterious luminous figure was photographed by a solicitor in a church in Arundel, Sussex, in 1940.

Below: A strange transparent figure appears in this picture of St Mary's Church, Woodford, Northamptonshire. Yet photographer Gordon Carroll says the church was empty.

league, Tim Newton. They used a computer programme designed to enhance photographic images and bring out hidden detail. One of the pictures subjected to their rigorous scrutiny was taken by a solicitor in a church in Arundel in the south of England in 1940. It shows a strange luminous figure in front of the altar. The computer quickly revealed the truth. The picture was in fact not one but a whole series of images. The experts' attention had been caught by the weird bright streak to the left of the figure. The computer showed that it was made up of a series of 'bumps', ending up at one of the altar candles. Significantly, when they measured the intervals between the 'bumps', Gull and Newton found they corresponded to the height of each step. Further investigations revealed that the figure had legs and was wearing a skirt. The answer was then obvious: the Arundel solicitor had managed to compress a whole sequence of events into one picture. What it showed was a woman walking up the altar steps carrying a taper which she had then used to light the altar candles.

In July 1964 Gordon Carroll, a clerk at a shoe factory in Northampton, spent his summer holiday touring local villages and photographing the scenery and architecture. One afternoon he set up his Ilford Sportsman Rangefinder camera on a tripod in St Mary's Church, in the village of Woodford, and took a photograph of the east window, the altar and choir stalls. Months later, when he was going through his slides, he noticed that there appeared to be a transparent figure kneeling on the altar steps. And yet he was sure the church had been empty when he had taken the picture. He considered the other possibilities. A double-exposure was unlikely, for the camera had a device to prevent this. Could it have been a trick of the light?

Was the 'figure' just a reflection from a window? This again was hardly possible: the angle of the sun would not have produced one in the right place at that time of the afternoon. Gordon Carroll concluded that only one chilling possibility remained: had he photographed a ghost?

The forensic computer's analysis produced a more mundane explanation. It revealed that Gordon Carroll's picture, like that of the Arundel solicitor, contained a whole sequence of images. When these had been separated, Dr Gull announced that the 'ghost' seemed to be a cleaning lady brushing the altar steps with a dustpan beside her. 'What seems to have happened here is that somebody in a very long exposure picture in a very dark church has been cleaning the step and moved several times during the course of the exposure.'

Gordon Carroll, it must be said, vigorously

Below: Mrs Mabel Chinery's snapshot of her husband Jim. Is the old lady in the back seat her mother, who died before the picture was taken?

disputes this suggestion. On learning of the computer's findings, he said,

> I was the only person in the church and there is no way a cleaner could have rushed in and out again without me noticing. At the time I even went up to the altar to the point where the figure showed up on the photograph, and took another picture of the other end of the church. There was definitely no one else there.

Finally, the computer examined a celebrated 'ghost' photograph taken in 1959 by a Suffolk woman, Mrs Mabel Chinery. It shows her husband Jim sitting in the driving seat of his car. Behind him, in the back, there appears to be an old lady wearing glasses and a scarf. According to Mrs Chinery, the lady looks just like her mother. Yet Mrs Chinery's mother had died before the picture was taken: in fact, it was the last frame of a film on which Mabel had photographed the old lady's grave. Mabel was certain that only Jim had been in the car: 'When I looked through the viewfinder all I saw was Jimmy in the car and snapped it and that was that.' So when the pictures had been processed and she recognized the distinctive features of her mother, Mabel was shocked: 'I felt dreadful,

I really did. I had to have a week off work. I couldn't believe it. I just couldn't believe it.'

As they pondered the mystery, Jim recalled his mother-in-law's words to him on the night before she died. Now they seemed eerily prophetic. 'The last thing she said to me when I went out of the room was, "Jim," she said, "you'll never come to any harm." She said, "I shall still be with you."'

The computer, however, had only the internal evidence of the photograph to work on, and it discerned several unusual features surrounding the mysterious old lady. Firstly, the light on the figure seemed to be coming from a different direction to that which illuminated the rest of the picture. Furthermore, her spectacles appeared to reflect more light than would have been available inside the car. Thirdly, the old lady did not seem to fit properly into the vehicle. For example, her shoulder could be seen to stretch beyond the pillar between the two windows, making her unnaturally broad. The experts therefore concluded that the picture was an accidental double-exposure, made up of the snapshot of Jim in his car and another very short exposure of Mabel's mother taken earlier.

Of course computers, like cameras, can lie, but the sad fact is that, although strange images on a few photographs *are* difficult to explain, not a single picture taken in 150 years of photography offers convincing proof of the existence of supernatural beings. The charming saga of the Cottingley fairies hoax and the more sinister exploits of the 'spirit' photographers tell us much about human credulity. The absence of unequivocal evidence from the millions upon millions of photographs taken since the invention of the camera may tell us even more about the nature of ghosts.

Arthur C. Clarke's own 'UFO photograph',
taken at the launch of Apollo 11 from Cape
Kennedy in July 1969.

Arthur C. Clarke comments:

Photography has been one of my major hobbies for more than fifty years; indeed, I lost my amateur status a long time ago, as half a dozen of my books have been illustrated by photographs I've taken above and below water. So the subject of this chapter is of particular interest to me. Though I've never captured a ghost on film, I *have* faked UFOs for a television programme, just to show how easily it can be done. And, by a coincidence so extraordinary I can still hardly believe it, I have two *unfaked* images on successive frames of 35-millimetre film of a most convincing UFO – hovering above the *Apollo 11* launch vehicle on the morning of 16 July 1969! I've never bothered to have them analyzed because it seemed unlikely that my camera alone, out of the several hundred thousand focused on that piece of Florida skyline, would have captured an inquisitive alien – though one would have been well-advised to keep an eye on humanity at that particular moment. (The images are almost certainly lens 'flares' caused by reflections from the sea of cars in the foreground.)

The story of the 'Cottingley fairies' is a tragi-comedy which, very conveniently, was resolved just in time for this book. The comic elements speak for themselves; the tragedy is that a man of Sir Arthur Conan Doyle's talents could so combine genius and utter stupidity, wasting time on an obvious hoax when he should have been usefully employed in Baker Street. And the story proves once again the truth of the old saying: 'Cameras can't lie – but liars can photograph.'

No picture in this book has a more compelling fascination than the photograph of the dead sailor buried beneath the Arctic ice for 140 years. The hands, manicured, immaculate as though they had just recently scrubbed the planked and caulked deck; the eyes open as if in life; the teeth shining. Only the forehead and nose show the blackening of frost. Lost in mysterious circumstances: Petty Officer John Torrington of the Franklin expedition. See page 165.

8.

Mysteries from East and West

This chapter is about three mysteries which have long fascinated us. Two of them, Spontaneous Human Combustion and the ability of eastern fakirs and pilgrims to withstand the pain of hooks and knives skewered into their flesh, are mentioned in our earlier books, but only briefly. We felt there was little new to say about them, and so, reluctantly, we moved on to consider phenomena upon which researchers *had* shed new light.

Later, we found that we had been mistaken. A letter from an English doctor convinced us that we should reopen our investigations into Spontaneous Human Combustion; while the answer to the hook hanging mystery lay virtually under our noses. It came – long after the *Strange Powers* book had gone to press but fortunately in time for the television series – from a distinguished professor of physiology who had conducted his experiments no more than a mile from Arthur C. Clarke's home in Colombo, Sri Lanka. He also had much to tell us about firewalking. A set of extraordinary photographs brought back from the Arctic in 1984 reminded us of the third mystery. Perhaps someone, somewhere, will write to explain it, too.

But first we must travel to the East . . .

Sri Lankan Superstition

When it comes to investigating the supernatural, the West now has no monopoly. The East, from whence so many mysteries have been reported by generations of marvelling travellers, has begun to produce its own psychical researchers. Few have been more assiduous or successful than two sceptics from Sri Lanka: one an outspoken maverick who devoted his life to the banishment of superstition; the other a respected professor of physiology who believes he can explain the most puzzling feats of the Oriental yogis – the ability to walk on fire and to hang from hooks without suffering serious injury.

On the morning of 13 May 1965 a terrified family gathered amidst the palm trees at the garden gate of a house at Karainagar near Jaffna, the northernmost town of Sri Lanka. They had come to greet a visitor from Colombo (far to the south) in the hope that he would rid them of a poltergeist which, they believed, had been turning their home and lives upside down for almost three months. They had been bombarded with stones which seemed to materialize inside the house, bruised by flying bottles and tins, and nauseated by the sand and dirt which used to appear suddenly in their rice at mealtimes. Money and possessions had gone missing, including keys, a leather bag and even a pair of false teeth left briefly on a stone by a well while their owner was having a wash. The family had also been plagued with illness since the onset of the sinister events.

The visitor was Dr Abraham Kovoor, then Sri Lanka's foremost psychical researcher, who had come to investigate. First, he walked round the outside of the house, pausing to admire the ornate satin-wood doors and peering into the out-house at the back where agricultural implements were stored. Then, Poirot-like, Kovoor set up his headquarters in the shed and turned his attention to the family: an elderly couple, their son and daughter, and the daughter's three girls,

Dr Abraham Kovoor, Sri Lanka's 'ghostbuster', investigates a case.

Devanayaki (thirteen), Sukirtham (eight) and four-year-old Selvamalar.

The adults were each questioned and their stories duly noted in Kovoor's casebook, but these interrogations were a formality: the psychic sleuth had already spotted the culprit. He wrote later:

> The fifth person to be questioned was the 13-year-old Devanayaki. Unlike the others who were questioned earlier, I adopted a different technique in dealing with her. I started with the assurance that I was in the know of what had happened in the house, and that I knew who was responsible for them. Without any hesitation, and with a smile on her face, Devanayaki explained to me in answer to my questions all that she had done during the previous two-and-a-half months.

Rajah the psychic parrot reading fortunes on a Colombo pavement.

The teenager had been responsible for all the 'poltergeist manifestations', with two exceptions: the disappearance of the false teeth, which had probably been snatched from the edge of the well by a passing crow, and the family illnesses, which were put down to coincidence. Dr Kovoor had simply used his powers of observation to crack the case. 'When I met all the members of the family as I stepped into the house first,' he said, 'I could spot out the poltergeist because Devanayaki's facial expressions betrayed her.' He had also noticed that the 'poltergeist' was never active between 9 am and 2 pm, the hours when Devanayaki was at school. Devanayaki, it turned out, had been jealous of her younger sister and, piqued by the lack of attention paid to her, had invented the 'poltergeist' to annoy the grown-ups. Dr Kovoor prescribed a course of deep hypnosis for the unhappy teenager and instructed her family to treat her with extra love and kindness. The result was that the poltergeist never reappeared. Devanayaki's family was rewarded with good marks from a model schoolgirl, and Dr Kovoor with a large Christmas hamper.

For Abraham Kovoor, however, it was simply another victory in his campaign against the superstitions which, he believed, reached right to the heart of life in Sri Lanka. Fortune-tellers still flourish throughout the island, even in the Fort of Colombo, the city's business district. Under the shady colonnade outside the Colombo Apothecaries store, for example, queues form early in the day at the stall of astrologer and palmist Miss Kosala Guneratna, who thoughtfully provides newspapers for her waiting clients to read. Near by, at 66⅓ Chatham Street, another astrologer, Mr B. Wettasinghe, uses a pocket calculator to compute the future. Throughout the Pettah, the city's teeming market area, more exotic seers ply their trade. In Jamahattha Street, Mrs P. Thiyagarajah gives 'light readings' by holding up a soot-blackened saucer to the sunlight and interpreting the patterns made on the surface by the dancing rays. Strangest of all, perhaps, are Rajah and Ranee, the psychic parrots, who hold their consultations on the pavement outside a Hindu temple. Upon payment of 1 rupee, the parrots' keeper fans out a pack of cards on the pavement in front of their wicker cage. Then he releases one of the birds, which scurries out and pecks one of the cards. On it, according to the parrot-keeper, his client's fate is written.

Many Sri Lankans consult astrologers be-

Below: A Sri Lankan *Kattadiya*, or witch doctor, prepares to consign an evil demon trapped in a bottle to the bottom of the Indian Ocean.

fore making important decisions. Patients have been known to postpone operations because the stars seem unfavourably aligned, and the horoscopes of prospective marriage partners are minutely compared to ensure compatibility. An ill-starred future can even mean the cancellation of marriage plans. Often, the times of important events are ordained according to the planetary conjunctions – even the opening ceremony of the futuristic Arthur C. Clarke Centre for Modern Technologies was carried out to a precise astrological schedule.

In the country districts, belief in demons is widespread, and *Kattadiyas,* the local variety of witch doctor, are hired to impose or exorcise curses. In one elaborate ceremony, regularly performed in the villages, the *Kattadiya* entices the evil demon from a 'possessed' person and, after a colourful

wrestling ritual, traps it in an empty bottle which is then consigned to the depths of the Indian Ocean, out of harm's way.

Such strong belief in the forces of the supernatural enraged Abraham Kovoor. 'Superstitions flourish on the ignorance and credulity of people,' he proclaimed, and he made it his business to debunk the beliefs of the 'gullibles', as he called them. Once, in India, he pretended that water from a railway station tap came from the holy river Ganges, and was delighted when 'many miraculous cures' were attributed to it. And he issued this challenge to the magicians and psychics:

> He who does not allow his miracles to be investigated is a crook, he who does not have the courage to investigate a miracle is a gullible, and he who is prepared to believe without verification is a fool. If there were a single person with supernatural powers in any part of the world, I would have become a pauper long ago because I have offered an award of one lakh [100,000] Sri Lanka rupees to anyone who can demonstrate any one of the 23 items of miracles mentioned in my permanent challenge under fraud-proof conditions. Though this open challenge was published all over the world some 15 years ago, I have not lost a single cent. Instead, I have gained a few thousands of rupees, the forfeited earnest deposits of contestants who failed to turn up in the end.

When Abraham Kovoor died in 1978, the reward was still on offer, and few claimants now come forward to be tested by his successor, Carlo Fonseka. Instead, Fonseka, Professor of Physiology at the University of Colombo, has been able to concentrate upon finding a rational explanation for those two Eastern mysteries which have fascinated and baffled travellers from the West since earliest times: fire walking and hook hanging.

Fire-walking

Fire-walking is regularly performed in Sri Lanka, both as a tourist attraction and as a religious ritual at festivals such as the annual pilgrimage to Kataragama, the island's holiest shrine. To conduct his investigation, Carlo Fonseka visited every fire-walk he could find and, with the eye of a trained medical man, watched the devotees as they crossed the burning coals. He wanted to answer a simple question: How can people walk on fire and not get burned? At each fire-walk, Fonseka began by measuring the distance travelled and the surface temperature. The longest fire-bed he found, at Kataragama, was 18 ft (5.5 m) long, while many were very much shorter. They were between 4 and 7 ft (1.2 to 2 m) wide, and the embers 3 to 6 in (8 to 15 cm) deep. Fire temperatures varied from about 300° to 450°C. More crucially, he timed the pilgrims as they crossed the coals and counted the number of steps they took. At Kataragama, the year the professor made his investigations, 100 walkers were on the fire for a mere 3 seconds on average. The fastest rushed across in only 1.5, and even the slowest traverse took just 6 seconds. Usually, walkers made it in ten steps, with the soles of their feet barely touching the coals – 0.3 seconds was the average time. These findings prompted Fonseka's first conclusion:

> At this stage an obvious question poses itself: is the immunity of fire-walkers from burns due to the shortness of the duration of contact between their soles and embers in taking a step? . . . If so, is it reasonable to suppose that those who get burnt as a result of fire-walking are in fact like the children little Alice in Wonderland had heard of, who got burnt all because they would not remember the simple rule that *'a red hot poker will burn you if you hold it too long?'*

But this could not be the whole answer: the casualty ward of the Kataragama hospital was grisly testimony to the fact that fire-walkers can suffer massive burns even after coming into contact with burning coals for only a few seconds. One British clergyman who braved the fire-pit – and ended up in the burns unit – later described the experience: 'It was like animals tearing at my feet,' he said.

Carlo Fonseka had also noticed another factor:

> Examination of the feet of the men who frequently do fire-walking showed that the epidermis of the soles of most of them was thick and rough when compared with that of habitually shod people. On being asked, most of them said that they never use any kind of foot-wear. Two obvious questions immediately suggested themselves: (1) are thick, rough soles more resistant to heat than thin, smooth ones? and (2) does habitual barefootedness increase the resistance of the soles to heat?

Back at the Medical Faculty, the professor knocked up an ingenious but simple apparatus, consisting of a 40-watt lightbulb in a metal cylinder. Volunteers, among them several experienced fire-walkers, were recruited for an experiment. Each of them simply put the sole of his foot on the top of the apparatus. Then Carlo Fonseka switched on the bulb and timed how long they were able to withstand its heat. The results showed a clear difference between the people who usually wore shoes and those who went round barefoot and whose soles had thickened as a result. In fact, the unshod 'guinea pigs' felt no heat at all for an average of 29 seconds and could keep their foot above the bulb for over 1¼ minutes, while those with soles softened by years of wearing shoes sensed the heat after only 6 seconds and were yelping in pain after 37. Further tests

Below: Professor Carlo Fonseka gives arrack, the
potent local spirit, to the firewalkers to demonstrate
that abstinence from alcohol is unnecessary for
successful firewalking.

showed that people with cold, wet feet could withstand the heat for even longer.

To confirm his hypotheses, Carlo Fonseka then ordered cartloads of logs – the *Vitex pinnata* regularly used in fire-walks. Next, he built a series of fifteen fires and carefully reproduced the conditions that obtained at Kataragama and other similar festivals. None of the laboratory walkers suffered burns, although the surface temperature of the fire-pit reached up to 500°C, but those with the softest feet had to skip speedily across the coals to avoid pain, while those with soles roughened by a lifetime of going barefoot were able to stroll across. The professor was delighted. Not only had his theories been borne out, but he could also dismiss as 'mumbo-jumbo' the widely held

idea that the ability to walk on hot coals was a supernatural power or a reward from divine authority for a good and moral life. 'Abstinence from meat, alcohol and sex is unnecessary to walk unscathed on fire,' he decided, and, in the interests of science, the firewalkers at the Medical Faculty defied religious convention by taking hearty swigs from a bottle of arrack, the potent local spirit, and devouring pork cutlets.

Hook-hangers

No sooner had Carlo Fonseka published the results of his fire-walking experiments in the *Ceylon Medical Journal* than a challenge from one of his own medical students sent him once more in search of fakirs and holy men. The student published an article in the

Below: Arthur C. Clarke watches a volunteer cross
burning coals during an experimental firewalk at the
University of Colombo Medical Faculty, Sri Lanka.

island's *Daily Mirror*. Though the headline
– HANGING ON HOOKS: WHAT IS THE EX-
PLANATION? – was rather bland, what he
had to say was provocative in the extreme –
at least to a rationalist professor of physiology.

He had been to religious festivals and was
amazed by the pilgrims who atoned for their
sins by hanging from ropes attached to their
bodies by razor-sharp hooks embedded in
their skin. The devotees' ability to withstand
pain and to survive their ordeal without any
apparent ill-effects seemed to the student to
defy medical science. 'Under normal conditions,' he wrote, 'these devotees are suscep-
tible to pain, bleeding, neurogenic shock,
tetanus, gas gangrene and bacterial infection
of wounds.' Yet none of these problems affec-

ted hook-hangers, nor did the hooks ever tear
their flesh, even when the full weight of their
bodies was suspended from ropes. He declared hook-hanging to be a miracle, for there
were, he said, seven inexplicable mysteries
about this 'fantastic feat of faith'.

Carlo Fonseka was not convinced. He was
ideally placed to investigate, for in Sri Lanka
there are professional hook-hangers who hire
themselves out for displays and tourist
shows. To them, a scientific experiment at
the Medical Faculty was all in a day's work.
From the many experts on offer, Professor
Fonseka chose 'a young rationalist-minded
volunteer named N. C. Jayasuriya' as his
'guinea pig'. Jayasuriya proved to be just the
man for the job and, in three long sessions of
carefully supervised investigation (for hook-

In Sri Lanka a volunteer hook-hanger is prepared for his ordeal. Before inserting the hooks, staff at Colombo University's Medical Faculty pinch up his skin to prevent bleeding.

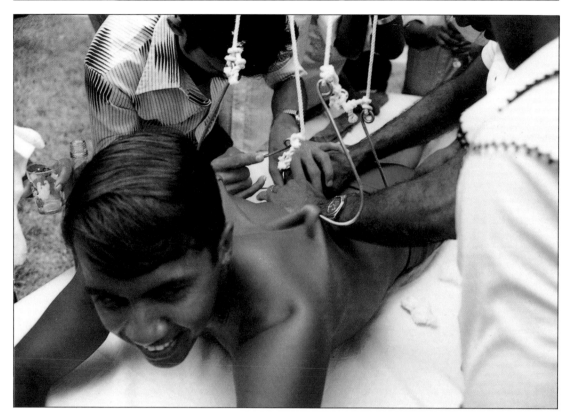

hanging, while not miraculous, can be highly dangerous to the uninitiated), became known as 'the Hero on Hooks'.

Carlo Fonseka examined each of the student's seven 'mysteries' in turn. His findings can be summarized in a series of questions and answers:

Question: Why does the hook-hanger appear to suffer no pain?

Answer: Because he has volunteered to undergo the ordeal. The right mental attitude is vital. Soldiers wounded in battle often say they feel no pain, and this may be because being wounded means they will be out of the combat zone for a time. For devotees, ecstasy and the feeling that they are purging their sins are powerful anaesthetics, but

even Mr Jayasuriya, who apparently 'spurned divine aid', suffered no agonies, simply because he had chosen to take part. In fact, he chattered happily to passers-by as he hung from the hooks during the experiments.

Question: Why do the hooks not make him bleed?

Answer: They do, but only a little. There are three reasons. Firstly, piercing the flesh releases the hormone adrenalin, which constricts the blood vessels in the skin and the superficial tissues into which the hooks are inserted. Secondly, the body has a natural mechanism (known as the 'extrinsic mechanism') for stopping bleeding from damaged tissues, which quickly comes into play and

The happy hook-hanger. The secret lies in a positive
mental attitude and the careful distribution of his
weight over several hooks.

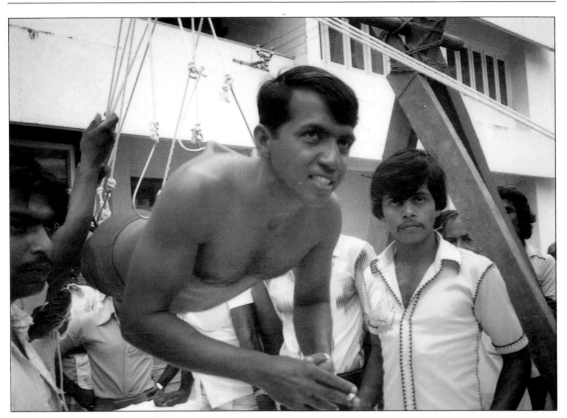

releases a chemical to clot the blood. The
third factor is perhaps the most important of
all: before the hook is inserted, the hanger's
assistants firmly pinch the place where it is
to go. This puts the surrounding blood vessels
out of action, and pressure from the rope to
which the hook is attached ensures that they
stay that way.

Question: How do they avoid tetanus, gas
gangrene and infected wounds?

Answer: They don't always. The problem
is that the devotees are seldom examined
later, but there is evidence that some wounds
do become infected. (During Fonseka's experiments the hooks and the wounds they produced were scrupulously wiped and sterilized.)
Tetanus and gangrene can be discounted, for

they are very rare, especially in the kind of
people who practise hook-hanging, who are
usually young and in good physical shape.

Question: Why doesn't the hook-hanger
faint during his ordeal?

Answer: People usually faint when they
are in great pain or when they are emotion-
ally upset. The hook-hanger is not in pain
and, far from being upset, is happy to be
doing penance in this spectacular way. (Mr
Jayasuriya, delighted to be of help in the
understanding of a 'miracle', did not faint
either.)

Question: Why don't the hooks tear the
hanger's back?

Answer: Because he hangs from several
hooks. One would certainly tear his flesh,

but several hooks distribute his weight and spread the load. Thus, if a devotee weighs 120 lbs (54 kilos) and uses six hooks, each one will have to bear only 20 lbs (9 kilos) – healthy human tissue can take the strain.

Carlo Fonseka is not only a rationalist: he is also a realist. He knows that however energetically he debunks the idea that hook-hanging and fire-walking are paranormal phenomena, people in his own country and abroad will probably continue to regard them as miracles. However, he continues his campaign undaunted, believing 'that it is intellectually degrading to continue to hold primitive beliefs which have become inconsistent with knowledge'. Indeed, so dedicated is he to his cause, that he has himself often walked on fire, each time emerging from the pit triumphant and, predictably, unburnt.

The Human Candles

Gruesome mysteries may require gruesome solutions. Thus it came about that a university professor, David Gee, could be found in his laboratory in Leeds fabricating a ghoulish test. First he rolled up a chunk of human body fat until it resembled an 8-in (24-cm) candle. Carefully he wrapped the 'candle' in a layer of human skin. Lastly, the whole object was clothed in fabric – dressed as though it were living flesh. Then Professor Gee applied a flame to the end of it.

He was ready to attempt to solve a mystery which has fascinated doctors and scientists for more than two centuries, and intrigued writers from Charles Dickens to Captain Marryat. Can human beings, apparently spontaneously, just burst into flame and melt away?

Professor Gee himself had been called to a case in Leeds in November 1963, when he was a young forensic scientist. He had found the remnants of an elderly woman, almost totally burned away apart from her right foot. Yet all around was undamaged combustible material. The hearth rug itself was intact except where the body had fallen. There was a tea towel, still neatly folded and scarcely singed, only a foot away from the body. The floorboards had burned through, but again only in the spot where the woman had fallen.

The young Dr Gee was intrigued. He knew that temperatures of 250°C or more were needed to make the human body burn. The precise Inquisitors of the Catholic Church had discovered that whole cartloads of wood were required to burn the heresy from recalcitrant souls and incinerate the bodies that had harboured such vice. Meaner allocations of fuel merely charred and roasted the sinner. In modern times, the annals of forensic science repeatedly demonstrate how futile it is for murderers to try to destroy the corpse of a victim by fire. Yet there are constant reports from unimpeachable sources of people being spontaneously, and for no apparent reason, consumed in flames.

A doctor from Aberdeen, Mackenzie Booth, recorded an astonishing case in which an old soldier had burned quietly away in a hayloft in Constitution Street in the middle of the city:

What struck me especially [he noted] was the fact that, notwithstanding the presence of abundant combustible material around, such as hay and wood, the main effects of combustion were limited to the corpse, and only a small piece of the adjacent flooring and the woodwork immediately above the man's head had suffered. The body was almost a cinder, yet retaining the form of the face and figure so well, that those who had known him in life could readily recognize him. Both hands and the right foot had been burnt off and had fallen through the floor among the ashes into the stables below. The hair and scalp were burnt off, exposing the bare and calcined skull. The tissues of the face were represented by a greasy cinder retaining the cast of the features, and the incinerated moustache still gave the wonted military expression to the old soldier.

Dr Booth was baffled.

Two years later, an American doctor was actually to witness 'spontaneous combustion' taking place. He was visiting a patient on the outskirts of the little town of Ayer, Massachusetts, when a girl rushed in begging him to come to her mother, who was being burned alive. The incident was only 200 yards away in some woodland. He arrived to find the woman's body still burning at the shoulder, along the trunk and down the legs.

'The flames reached from twelve to fifteen inches above the level of the body,' he reported. 'The clothing was nearly all consumed. As I reached the spot, the bones of the right leg broke with an audible snap, allowing the foot to hang by the tendons and muscles of one side, those of the other side having burned completely off.' Yet, bizarrely, except where the body had actually been burning, the mother's clothes were untouched. A woollen skirt, a cotton vest, a calico dress, underclothes, had all survived in parts unburnt. All around, the ground was untouched apart from a few charred leaves under the corpse, and her straw hat, slightly scorched, a few feet away. The woman had been out in the woods, clearing stumps and undergrowth, and had indeed started a fire which might have caught her clothing. But that in no way seemed to Dr Hartwell to explain the human incendiary which he had seen before his very eyes.

Both these cases are nearly a century old.

Yet incidents keep recurring which confound the results of another 100 years of research into the properties of flame.

Fireman Jack Stacey was called to an incident in a run-down part of Vauxhall, South London, at Christmas 1967. A fire was reported. When the fire engine arrived, the crew found some down-and-outs awaiting them. They had been using an old building. Inside was the body of another vagrant. Said Mr Stacey, 'It was still alight. There were flames coming from the abdomen. They were coming out of a four-inch slit in the abdomen. It was a bluish flame. It seemed as though the fire had begun inside the body.' The building itself was undamaged, although there was charring of the woodwork underneath the victim.

At the end of 1985 the BBC showed a programme in which a police officer, John Haymer, testified to a strange death in South Wales in 1979. When he arrived at the house he was immediately struck by an orange-red glow in the main room.

> The walls were generating heat. The window and lightbulb were covered in an orange substance. The lightbulb was bare because the plastic shade had melted. The settee still had its loose covers. The carpet was largely undamaged.
>
> On the floor was a pair of human feet clothed in socks. They were attached to the lower portion of the body. This was clad in trousers, undamaged as far as a distinct burn line. From the trousers protruded the calcined bone. And just beyond the knees, this disintegrated into an amorphous mass of ash.

The debris was all that remained of the elderly man who had lived in the house. Haymer was puzzled enough at the almost total destruction of the body, but what was even more baffling was the lack of damage elsewhere. The TV set was still on, though its

All that remained of Dr John Irving Bentley,
Pennsylvania, December 1966.

Below: Jacqueline Fitzsimon who was 'engulfed in flame' while walking down the college stairs.

plastic control knobs had melted. The grate itself was undisturbed, with unburnt firewood still in place. No cause of death, no source for the fire was ever found. Haymer, a sober individual who had investigated many deaths and had never flirted with the paranormal, believes to this day that the case defies rational explanation.

These modern cases of bodies reduced to ash in unscorched surroundings are the more incomprehensible to investigators because the technology of consuming a corpse in fire is now well understood as a result of the advancing fashion for cremation in both Britain and America. Crematoria have become remarkably sophisticated and automated, now that most people choose to have their earthly remains rapidly obliterated. The ovens which do the job operate at temperatures of at least 800°C and, even after an hour or more, quite large fragments of bone will remain. Rarely is there the complete reduction to ash which is a feature of the 'spontaneous combustion' cases.

These burnings are not usually witnessed, and there is only circumstantial evidence as to how long the process takes. But even in modern times there are cases of the most spectacular and horrible form of 'spontaneous combustion', when people burst into flames in front of friends, families or passers-by. These are the cases which have truly horrified, rather than merely intrigued, those unfortunate enough to see them – a man so angry during a dispute with a neighbour that he simply exploded into flame; in 1973 a baby who was suddenly alight in his pram; the six Nigerians in 1976 all consumed in a fire which hardly damaged their room. These dramas have all surfaced in the newspapers with neither explanation nor serious investigation.

However, in the winter of 1985 there was a dreadful incident in Cheshire, which was investigated at first hand by police, fire officers, a forensic chemist working for the British Home Office, and by the prestigious Shirley Institute in Manchester. A seventeen-year-old student, Jacqueline Fitzsimon, was walking down some stairs with a group of friends at Halton College of Further Education, Widnes, when she suddenly burst into flame. Although three staff members quickly arrived on the scene and smothered the flames, Jacqueline subsequently died.

Witnesses under oath at the inquest described the events of that February morning in apocalyptic terms. Two girls, Carina Leazer and Rachel Heckle, had passed Jacqueline on the stairs. Carina told the coroner that she noticed a strange glowing light above Jacqueline's right shoulder. It appeared in mid-air and then seemed to fall down her back. Two men, both mature

students, were also on the stairs. John Foy, aged thirty-four, who worked for a chemical manufacturer, described hearing Jacqueline cry out. They turned to see her on fire. 'She was like a stunt man on TV,' he said. 'The flames simply engulfed her.' He and his companion, Neil Gargan, had seen no sign of smoke or smouldering as they passed the girl just a few seconds before. They helped put out the fire. Jacqueline herself only complained that she had burnt her finger trying to put out the flames, though there was melted nylon all over her back. She died in hospital.

Initially there seemed to be a fairly simple explanation. Jacqueline was a cookery student and had been working in the cookery room where a number of gas cookers were in use. She had finished her work early and had stood about talking to friends. The assumption was that she had perhaps leaned against a cooker where the gas ring was still on, her white catering jacket had started to smoulder and then, when she went out to the stairway, the increased oxygen and air-flow had fanned it into flame.

Slowly, however, doubts began to build up about this straightforward theory. There had been plenty of people about and no one had noticed any sign of scorching or smouldering on Jacqueline's back. Indeed, she had walked down the stairs linking arms with two friends, and they had not noticed anything. Then the cookery lecturer, Robert Carson, swore that all the rings had been turned off an hour before the end of the study period. 'In any case,' he told the coroner, 'in twenty years I have never seen a catering jacket on fire.' Next, the Home Office chemist, Philip Jones, described how he had been unable to make a smouldering catering jacket burst into flames, even when it was exposed to a strong air-flow. The Shirley Institute report

also acknowledged that they could not get a smouldering catering jacket to flame. If it was directly ignited the whole thing burned within twenty-five seconds. Yet all the evidence indicated that a considerable time – several minutes – had elapsed between Jacqueline's departure from the cookery room and the fatal conflagration on the stairs.

The jury's verdict was 'Misadventure'. But few people, either among the witnesses or among those who had attended the inquest, felt that they had heard a satisfactory explanation of why a seventeen-year-old girl should, without warning, be consumed by fire while walking downstairs arm-in-arm with friends one February morning.

The most relentlessly investigated case of modern times was the death of sixty-seven-year-old widow, Mary Reeser, in St Petersburg, Florida, in 1951. Her son, Dr Richard Reeser, had last seen her sitting in an armchair reading as he left for an evening out. When he returned there was nothing left of the chair except the metal springs. Of his mother there remained only her left foot, bizarrely unscorched, a few pieces of backbone and, apparently, a skull shrunk to the size of a baseball. The room was covered in oily soot, and a pair of candles 12 ft (3.5 m) away from the body had melted. Yet newspapers and linen only inches away were intact. The room was stiflingly hot.

The local fire chief, Jake Reichert, confessed that it was the 'most unusual case I've seen in my almost twenty-five years of police work'.

Dr Wilton Krogman of the University of Pennsylvania reported the circumstances. He noted that not only was it peculiar that the fire was so localized and yet had clearly generated great heat, but also that there

The remains of Mrs M. H. Reeser are sifted in
St Petersburg, Florida, July 1951.

was an odd absence of smell. 'How could a
hundred and seventy pounds of mortal flesh
burn with no detectable or discernible smoke
or odor permeating the entire apartment
building?' Krogman remarked on the
shrunken skull, 'I have experimented on this
using cadaver heads,' but no similar effect
had ever been produced.

Arson specialist Edward Davies was des-
patched by the National Board of Under-
writers to analyse the death. He could find
no cause.

More than thirty years later, two investigators, Joe Nickell and John F. Fischer, re-
worked the evidence for the *Journal of the
International Association of Arson Investi-*

gators and came to the conclusion that Mary Reeser had taken sleeping pills and had probably set herself and the chair alight with a cigarette. They dismissed the shrunken skull as it was reported only by Dr Krogman, who did not claim to have seen it for himself.

However, the great heat, the undamaged flammable material all around, the unburnt foot all remain as imponderables in Mary Reeser's death.

Ever since the drive towards 'science and enlightenment' began three centuries ago, there have been repeated attempts to explain a phenomenon which has regularly attracted the attention of journals and physicians.

Pierre-Aimé Lair produced an *'Essai sur les Combustions Humaines'* for the Paris medical publishers Crapelet in 1800. Most of the examples he cited were culled from the British *Annual Register* and the *Transactions of the Royal Society*. He describes the expiry of Grace Pitt from Ipswich, who died in April 1744. She was found by her daughter, who threw two vases of water over her. All that remained was what Lair described as a carpet of ash with some white cinders. He also cites the 1779 report by a surgeon, Muraire, from Aix-en-Provence. A widow, Marie Jauffret, 'small, fat and fond of the bottle', had burnt away to a cinder, leaving 'one hand, one foot and the bones of the skull' unconsumed.

Lair was primarily concerned to show that over-indulgence in 'spiritous liquors' was responsible for spontaneous combustion. His theory was that most of the victims he recorded had been fat and addicted to alcohol. The alcohol, he opined, would build up in their tissues until finally they exploded into flame – rather, one assumes, like burning brandy on a Christmas pudding.

This prognosis – popular, naturally, among temperance campaigners – remained the favoured solution for the best part of a century, while the list of victims of the 'heavenly fire' steadily increased.

There are now hundreds of cases, many photographs, reliable witnesses, medical and forensic testimony, all demonstrating that human beings can be reduced to ash. Many show the most grotesque features of 'spontaneous combustion' – a hand or a foot left behind without a mark. Invariably, although there are signs of great heat, combustible materials near the body have been untouched. Usually there is no obvious source of fire – certainly not sufficient to generate crematorium levels of heat. Sadly for Pierre-Aimé Lair and his successors, there is by no means always evidence of an addiction to strong drink.

It was against this background that Professor Gee of Leeds began his ghoulish but necessary experiment with a human candle. Gee knew that human body fat, even when melted down in a crucible, will only burn at a temperature of about 250°C. However, a cloth wick in liquid fat will burn like a lamp when the temperature is as low as 24°C. With this in mind, Gee constructed his human candle wrapped in layers of cloth. He then set a bunsen burner at one end. It took about a minute for the fat to catch fire. As his report dispassionately records:

> Although the bunsen was removed at this point, combustion of the fat and cloth proceeded slowly along the length of the roll, with a smoky yellow flame and much production of soot, the entire roll being consumed after about one hour. In the experiment the draught of air from an extractor fan was arranged so that combustion proceeded in a direction opposite to the flow of air.

Another forensic professor, Keith Mant,

summed up the current state of scientific thinking in the 1984 edition of *Taylor's Principles and Practice of Jurisprudence.*

> It seems that the probable course of events in these cases is that the victim collapses, for instance from a heart attack, or from carbon monoxide poisoning, and falls so that part of the body comes into contact with a source of heat such as a small domestic fire. This part of the body, usually the head, is thus ignited, and adjacent body fat when melted soaks into the layers of clothing, which, the victim being an old lady, are likely to be present in abundance. The clothing, acting as a wick, melts the next zone of adjacent fat, and the process is repeated along the length of the body. If floorboards beneath the body are ignited, they will be burnt through, and the sudden increase in draught which results will considerably raise the temperature and incinerate the rest of the body. By the time the lower legs are reached there is less fat and few, if any, layers of clothing, so the process ceases.

The scenario is as plausible as the evidence allows. But for the sceptic there remain ample imponderables. Can such great heat be generated as to pulverize bone too, and yet not burn surrounding combustibles – cloth, paper, even hay and straw? What about flames coming out of the victim's stomach? What about those fearful cases where people catch light suddenly in front of friends and passers-by? What about the shrunken skull?

The manifestations of the heavenly fire still throw up questions which have not yet proved amenable to the inquests of the laboratory and the bunsen burner.

Arthur C. Clarke comments:

The *Strange Powers* television programme devoted to fire-walking and religious rituals such as hanging on hooks was broadcast in Sri Lanka (where much of it had been filmed) on 17 October 1986. I had rather hoped that my – and still more, Professor Carlo Fonseka's – 'debunking' of fire-walking would promote the ire of the professionals. Not a bit of it. In fact the only local criticism I received was from Mr A. C. B. M. Moneragala of Kelaniya (not far from Colombo, and the site of a famous Buddhist temple). He complained that we didn't do a thorough *enough* job of rationalizing, and enclosed an article he had published in the *Ceylon Daily News* for 16 October 1981, entitled 'Natural Pain Killers'. This discussed the recently discovered natural opiate, beta-endorphin, which the body appears to produce in direct proportion to the severity of the pain suffered.

To quote from Mr Moneragala's article:

> Apparently, powerful and awesome religious emotions are able to release this natural narcotic . . . controlling both physical and mental pain . . . In the presence of death and in the fearsome havoc of the battlefield beta-endorphin is released into the limbic area of the brain and gruesome injuries and death are faced with apparent indifference . . . [When] one of Napoleon's generals had his legs badly shattered by a cannonball they were amputated on the battlefield itself, without an anaesthetic and then thrust into a cauldron of boiling tar to be disinfected. All this time the general showed no sign of pain. His only antidote was his cigar which he smoked continually during this ghastly butchery . . .

I have little doubt that some such explanation is correct – and quite marvellous. All we have to do now is to explain the explanation. And that is a matter of no small importance, for it may lead to results of immeasurable value to the human race – the Conquest of Pain.

As for the 'human candles', in the Introduction to *Arthur C. Clarke's Mysterious World* I classified mysteries into three categories,

'. . . is it the cinder of a small charred and broken log of wood with white ashes, or is it coal? O Horror, he IS here!' Charles Dickens' *Bleak House*, the first fictional account of spontaneous human combustion.

according to our current level of understanding:

> Mysteries of the Third Kind [I wrote] are the rarest of all, and there is very little that can be said about them . . . They are phenomena – or events – for which there appears to be *no* rational explanation; in the cases where there are theories to account for them, these are even more fantastic than the 'facts'.
>
> Perhaps the quintessential M3K is something so horrible that – even if the material existed – one would prefer not to use it in a television programme. It is the extraordinary phenomenon known as Spontaneous Human Combustion.
>
> There have been many recorded cases, supported by what seems to be indisputable medical evidence, of human bodies being consumed in a very short period of time by an extremely intense heat *which has often left the surroundings – even the victim's clothing! – virtually untouched.* The classic fictional case is in Dickens' *Bleak House*, but there are dozens of similar incidents in real life – and probably a far greater number that have never been reported.

The human body is not normally a fire hazard; indeed, it takes a considerable amount of fuel to arrange a cremation. There seems no way in which this particular mystery can ever be solved without a great deal more evidence – and who would wish for that?

Well, since I wrote those words, more evidence has – tragically – become available. And I am indebted to Dr Geoffrey Diggle of Croydon for reference to experiments that suggest that, in his words, 'this previously baffling phenomenon has now been elucidated and shown not to require any preternatural explanation. In other words, the M3K had graduated to an M1K!'

I am still not completely convinced, despite the experiments which have been conducted in attempts to solve this bizarre mystery. I know of nothing else in the whole range of 'paranormal' literature that gives me such a feeling of unease. Some of the evidence seems beyond dispute – yet, if accepted, it hints that there *are* forces in the universe of which we know nothing. And even that there may be something in the old horror movie cliché: 'Such knowledge is not meant for Man . . .'

Here is a somewhat lighter, perfectly genuine and possibly relevant item from the *British Medical Journal* for 12 December 1964.

> I recall a case referred to me many years ago. The patient was a parson who became alarmed when he noticed that his breath took fire every time he blew the altar candles out. I performed a Polya-gastrectomy for a duodenal ulcer causing pyloric stenosis, following which he was able to carry out his duties in a more decorous fashion – I am, etc., Stephen Power, Royal London Homeopathic Hospital.

Below: Her Majesty's ships *Erebus* and *Terror* before they set sail, loaded with provisions for three years.

The Ships in the Ice

No picture in this book has a more compelling fascination than the photograph at the beginning of this chapter. It shows a dead sailor buried beneath the Arctic ice for 140 years. The hands, manicured, immaculate as though they had just recently scrubbed the planked and caulked deck; the eyes open as if in life; the teeth shining. Only the forehead and nose show the blackening of frost. The corpse is as perfect as that of the baby mammoth found in the Soviet north just five years before. It seems as if only some special stroke of lightning from out of the tundran sky would be needed to re-animate the young man in his icy coffin.

These pictures (brought back from Beechey Island in Canada's Barrow Strait, far beyond the Arctic Circle, in the summer of 1984) are, however, merely the latest clue to the greatest enigma of Arctic exploration – the fate of Sir John Franklin and his ships after they entered the northern ice in the summer of 1845.

The dead seaman is Petty Officer John Torrington. He was only nineteen years old when he sailed with Franklin to try to find the North West Passage from the Atlantic to the Pacific, which had eluded explorers for two centuries. Professor Owen Beattie of the University of Alberta, who exhumed Torrington and also Able Seaman John Hartnell, said: 'The bodies were extremely

Captain Sir John Franklin, leader of the expedition in
1845 to find the North West Passage.

life-like, with skin almost normal and hair intact. It was a very touching experience. We felt very close to a moment of history.' Professor Beattie was leading the latest of scores of expeditions which have tried to solve the Franklin mystery. At one time, in the summer of 1850, there were no less than ten ships searching for Franklin. Bodies have been discovered, cairns, even messages left behind, but the two ships *Erebus* and *Terror* have never been found, and many of the clues merely seem to add to the mystery.

Franklin was already sixty years old when he left Britain in May 1845. The ships had provisions for three years, as it was expected that they would be imprisoned in the ice for at least one winter, perhaps two. After calling in on the west Greenland coast, they were last seen by the whaler *Enterprise* leaving Melville Bay. None of the 129 crew of the two ships were ever seen alive again. But the deaths of Torrington, Hartnell, and Marine William Braine so early in the expedition – they appear to have died of either scurvy or lead poisoning – less than a year after they set sail, only add to the puzzles of a baffling expedition.

Subsequent expeditions found two messages left behind on King William Island. One reported that *Erebus* and *Terror* had wintered in 1846–7 at Beechey Island. The second message read:

April 25 1848. HM's ships *Terror* and *Erebus* were deserted on 22nd April, 5 leagues NNW of this, having been beset since 12 September 1846. The officers and crew, consisting of 105 souls, under the command of Capt. F. R. M. Crozier, landed here in Lat 69 37 42 N Long 98 41 W.

Sir John Franklin died on 11 June 1847, and the total loss by deaths in the expedition has been to this date 9 officers and 15 men.

Signed James Fitzjames, Captain *HMS Erebus*
F. R. M. Crozier, Captain and Senior Officer.

and start on tomorrow, 26th., for Back's Fish River.

Later, more than a dozen bodies were found further south at Starvation Cove.

Then, bizarrely, further north and facing out to sea, an extraordinary catafalque was discovered – a full-size ship's boat, mounted on a massive sledge with iron-shod runners, and, in it, two bodies, equipped like some Chinese emperor for the afterworld. Each had a double-barrelled gun with one barrel loaded and cocked. With them were calf-skin slippers, edged with red silk ribbon. One skeleton was wrapped in furs. There was a complete set of dinner plates with Sir John Franklin's crest and silver knives, forks and spoons with the crests or initials of five of *Erebus*'s officers and three of *Terror*'s. There were books, towels, soap, silk handkerchiefs, and 'an amazing quantity of clothing'. And all this facing back towards the frozen sea. What was the meaning of this extraordinary caravanserai, setting out so caparisoned after three years alone in the Arctic? Why was the mighty sledge-boat facing back towards the sea? Why had nine officers died – such a high proportion? Above all, what had happened to the ships? Not a nail or a plank has ever been found in all the years of searching for Franklin.

Could it possibly be true that the ships were seen high and dry on an iceberg off the Newfoundland banks, as three mariners aboard the brig *Renovation* reported in April 1851? This was 2,000 miles away from where the ships were abandoned. It seems unthinkable. But then one of the ships searching for Franklin, the *Resolute*, was found sailing

Giant icebergs drift thousands of miles from the North West Passage.

like the *Mary Celeste* in Baffin Bay, 1,000 miles from where she had been prematurely deserted by her crew. The *Resolute* was picked up and taken to New London, Connecticut, where she was refitted and returned, courtesy of the United States Congress, to the British Admiralty. And there is little reason to doubt the evidence of the voyagers aboard the *Renovation,* which was in passage from Limerick in Ireland to Quebec in the spring of 1851.

The first account appeared in a letter from John S. Lynch published in the *Limerick Chronicle*:

> The icebergs we met with were frightful in size. I do not exaggerate when I say that the steeple of Limerick cathedral would have appeared but a small pinnacle, and a dark one compared to the lofty and gorgeously-tinted spires that were on some of them. We met, or rather saw at a distance, one with two ships on it.

Later, Lynch was interrogated by the Admiralty. He told Captains Herbert and Boxer, RN, who were investigating, that the *Renovation* had been off the Newfoundland banks.

> We came in view of one iceberg, on which I distinctly saw two vessels, one certainly high and dry, the other might have her keel and bottom in the water, but the ice was a long way outside of her. I examined them particularly with the spy glass; one, the larger, lay on her beam ends, the other upright. I said to the mate that they were part of Sir J. Franklin's squadron. He said very likely, and that it would be a good prize for whoever would fall in with them. My reason for supposing them to belong to Sir John Franklin's squadron was there being two ships on one iceberg, they appearing to be consorts, and having no appearance of being driven on the berg in distress, as the rigging and the spars of the upright one was all as shipshape as if she had been laid up in

CAPTAIN CROZIER. ("TERROR.")

CAPTAIN SIR JOHN FRANKLIN, K.H.C.

COMMANDER FITZJAMES, (CAPTAIN,—"EREBUS.")

LIEUT. COUCH. (MATE.)

LIEUT. FAIRHOLM.

C. H. OSMER. (PURSER.)

LIEUT. DES VŒUX. (MATE.)

LIEUT. GRAHAM GORE. (COMMANDER.)

S. STANLEY. (SURGEON.)

LIEUT. H. T. D. LE VESCONTE.

LIEUT. R. O. SARGENT. (MATE.)

JAMES REID, (ICE MASTER.)

H. D. S. GOODSIR. (ASSISTANT-SURGEON.)

COLLINS, (2ND MASTER.)

Left: The officers of *Erebus* and *Terror*, all of whom perished on the fated expedition.

Below: Robert Simpson's sketch of the two ships on the iceberg, from the *Nautical Magazine* of 1852.

harbour; also the one on her beam ends had no more appearance of a wreck than a vessel with her topmast struck and left by the tide on a beach, no loose ropes hanging from any part of her.

The captain of the *Renovation* was sick at the time and would not countenance going any closer to the iceberg. But Lynch was quite clear that he had not seen an optical illusion: 'Having seen them in different positions and minutely, I can have no doubt upon the subject at all.'

Later, the second mate of the *Renovation*, Robert Simpson, was questioned. He produced a vivid sketch, which was published in the *Nautical Magazine* of 1852, and confirmed the details of Lynch's account. He estimated the ships' size as between 4,000

and 5,000 tons for the larger and perhaps 100 tons less for the smaller. Both the rig and the deck array of the ships coincided with the appearance of *Erebus* and *Terror*.

It seems clear that all Franklin's crew perished in the vain attempt to reach the Canadian mainland at Fish River. The details of his attempted route, which indeed was accepted as proof of the existence of the North West Passage, are now clear. Professor Beattie may soon, from his analysis, know what caused Petty Officer Torrington's death – possibly lead poisoning from the early tinned food cans. But what happened to *Erebus* and *Terror* themselves is as mysterious as it was 140 years ago. The sledge-boat on King William Island remains one of the eeriest wrecks in all history.

Arthur C. Clarke, Chancellor of the University of Moratuwa, Sri Lanka, before delivering the annual Convocation address.

9.

Where Are They?

Arthur C. Clarke writes:

One morning in 1979 I opened the local morning paper to be greeted with the news, CLARKE TO HEAD UNIVERSITY. 'How interesting,' I thought. 'I wonder who that can be – I don't know any other Clarkes in Sri Lanka . . .' Then I read on, and was both astonished and flattered to learn that President J. R. Jayawardene had appointed me Chancellor of our leading technical institution, the University of Moratuwa, about five miles south of Colombo.

Fortunately for the educational system of Sri Lanka, the Chancellor is not involved in the day-to-day running of the university, and his main duty is to present the graduates with their degrees and give a suitably inspiring address at the annual Convocation. Each year I try to find a new subject, and it so happened that in 1986 I came back to one that – inevitably – took up a whole programme in the *Mysterious World* television series, as well as Chapter 10 of the associated book. (How odd: I've just noticed that whereas there were thirteen parts to the series, the book has only twelve chapters. Have my co-authors become superstitious as a result of investigating too many mysteries?)

Over the last forty years I have written quite a number of essays on UFOs and on life in outer space – two subjects which are not necessarily connected. In the aftermath of Halley's Comet, which focused so much attention on matters astronomical, the time seemed ripe for a summing-up. I attempted to do this in my Chancellor's Address, delivered in the splendid Bandaranaike Memorial International Hall, Colombo, on 20 June 1986.

I sincerely hope I can now give the whole subject a few decades of benign neglect, but from previous experience I'm not too optimistic. All I can say is that these are my Latest Last Words on UFOs.

Early in December 1985 a group of distinguished astronomers gathered in Colombo – under the auspices of the International Astronomical Union, the Institute of Fundamental Studies, and the Arthur C. Clarke Centre – to discuss a subject which has long fascinated the general public, but which has only become scientifically respectable during the last two decades. I refer, of course, to the possibility of life on other worlds.

Now, this is a fairly new idea in Western thought – for the simple reason that from Aristotle onwards it was assumed that the earth was the centre of the universe and that anything beyond it was some vague celestial realm inhabited only by supernatural beings. The sun was obviously a mass of fire, so no one except the gods could live *there*, and as for the moon, it probably wasn't big enough for many occupants. The five planets visible to the naked eye – Mercury, Venus, Mars, Jupiter, Saturn – had been known to mankind since prehistoric times, and their curious movements had been the cause of much speculation. But no one except a few eccentric philosophers had any idea that they were all worlds in their own right – two of them enormously larger than the earth.

It's an extraordinary fact that the East had guessed the true scale of the universe, both in time and in space, centuries before the West. In Hindu philosophy there are aeons and ages long enough to satisfy any modern cosmologist; yet until only a dozen generations ago much of Europe believed that the world was created around 4000 BC. (I'm sorry to say that, owing to their misreading of the Bible, thousands of foolish people still believe such nonsense.) The turning point in our understanding of the universe may be conveniently dated at 1600, just before Galileo pointed his first telescope towards the stars. Shakespeare belongs to the century before the great intellectual revolution.

> Doubt that the stars are fire,
> Doubt that the sun doth move . . .

he wrote, circa 1600. He was wrong on both counts.

Of course, we know that the sun *does* move – but not in the way that Shakespeare imagined. He thought it moved around the earth, as common sense seems to indicate, and had no idea how distant – and how big – it really is. And the stars aren't fire – although for reasons that were not understood until well into this century. They are much too hot! Fire is a *low*-temperature phenomenon in the thermal range of the universe – much of which is simmering briskly at several million degrees, where no chemical compounds can possibly exist.

During the seventeenth century the telescope revealed for anyone who had eyes to see that the moon provided at least one other example of a world with mountains and plains – though not rivers and oceans. The moving points of light that were the planets now turned out to have appreciable discs – and one of them, Jupiter, had its own retinue of moons. Clearly, the earth was not unique; nor, perhaps, was the human race.

This was a shocking – even heretical – thought, at least to those brought up in the Aristotelean school. Anyone who preached it too loudly, especially near Rome, was likely to get into serious trouble with the Inquisition. The classic example is, of course, Giordano Bruno (1548—1600), who was one of the first European advocates of the doctrine of an infinite universe and the 'plurality of worlds'. Refusing to recant, he was burned at the stake in 1600. I wonder how many modern scientists would be prepared to emulate him in defence of their theories.

A couple of years ago, to my great surprise, I was asked to present a paper to the Pontifical Academy of Science, and could not resist having a little dig at the Vatican Astronomer.

'When I was invited to speak here,' I told Dr George Coyne mischievously, 'my first choice of subject was: "After Giordano Bruno – Who?"'

George didn't hesitate for a moment. 'If you had used that title, Arthur,' he said deadpan, 'the answer would have been – "*You*."'

And while we're on the subject of Jesuit astronomers, I'd like to remind you of one of the greatest ironies in the history of science. In 1582 that remarkable man, Father Matteo Ricci, arrived in China with all the latest wisdom of the West. The Chinese regarded Occidentals as barbarians (and probably still do, though they're too polite to say so), but by tact, intelligence and sheer goodness Father

Giordano Bruno, the Italian philosopher who was
burned at the stake in 1600 for his 'heretical' ideas
about the universe.

Below: Father Matteo Ricci. A remarkable Jesuit
missionary, but his misguided astronomical theories
were a mixed blessing to the Chinese.

Ricci persuaded them that their superstitious concept of an enormous universe enduring for vast aeons was all nonsense: God
put the earth in the centre of everything, and
Adam and Eve in the garden, only a few
thousand years ago. As he proudly wrote:
'The Fathers gave such clear and lucid explanation on all these matters which were so
new to the Chinese, that many were unable
to deny the truth of all that they said; and, for
this reason, the information on this matter
quickly spread among all the scholars of
China.' Well! Poor Father Ricci! While he
was persuading the Chinese to take a Great
Leap Backward to Ptolemaic astronomy,
Copernicus was destroying its very foun-
dations in Europe. A few decades later Galileo (with an anxious glance over his shoulder
at Bruno) would finish the job of demolition.

For the last 300 years – not very long in
human history – all educated persons have
known that our planet is not the only world
in the universe, and that its sun is one of
billions. The great voyages of the seventeenth and eighteenth centuries, during
which European explorers 'found' whole cul-
tures that didn't even know they'd been lost,
also prompted speculation about life on other
planets. It seemed only reasonable that our
enormous cosmos must be populated with
other creatures, some of them perhaps far
more advanced than we are. The alternative
– that we are utterly alone in the universe –
seemed both depressing and wildly megalo-
maniac.

But how to prove it, one way or the other?
We children of the Space Age can no longer
remember how enormous even the solar system seemed, only a lifetime ago. Now the
Voyager spaceprobe is heading for its appointment with Neptune – which, as recently
as 1930, marked the frontier of the Empire of

the Sun. That is an impressive achievement;
even so, it will be tens of thousands of years
before *Voyager* can cross the gulf to the nearest star.

Fortunately, we do not have to rely on
physical contact to discover if there is intelligent life elsewhere in the universe. We now
assume that any contact is likely to be by
radio. Yet this in itself would have seemed
incredible until well into this century. We
take radio so much for granted that we forget
how miraculous it is. Even the most far-
sighted prophet could not have predicted it –
which is yet another example of what I call
Comte's Fallacy.

Around 1840 the French philosopher,
Auguste Comte (1798–1857), was rash
enough to make the following pronounce-
ment about the limits of our knowledge con-

Below: Auguste Comte. His *gaffe* was to set limits to
man's knowledge of the heavenly bodies.

cerning the heavenly bodies: 'We see how we may determine their forms, their distances, their bulk, their motions, but we can never know anything of their chemical or mineralogical structure; and much less, that of organized beings living on their surface.' Comte's monumental *gaffe* was in the same class as Father Ricci's. Within a few decades, the invention of the spectroscope had utterly refuted his assertion that it was impossible to discover the chemical nature of heavenly bodies. By the end of the century, precisely *that* was the main occupation of most professional astronomers. Only the amateurs were still concerned with what Comte believed must always be the entire body of their science.

So it is very dangerous to set limits to knowledge or to engineering achievements.

No one could have anticipated the spectroscope; and no one could have imagined radio. They both exemplify Clarke's well-known Third Law: 'Any sufficiently advanced technology is indistinguishable from magic.'

There may be 'magical' inventions or discoveries in the future which will settle the question of intelligent life in the universe, but I do not think we really need them. Today's electronics can probably do the job – given a few more decades of determined application. The giant radio telescopes which have been built for purely scientific purposes are quite capable – and this is a splendid example of 'serendipity' – of detecting the sort of radio signals one would expect from an advanced civilization in our immediate galactic neighbourhood. As is well known, a number of such searches have been made – and are being made right now – though so far with negative results. It would be ridiculously optimistic to expect success, since we have had the capacity for making such a search for less than half a human lifetime.

Yet already this 'failure' has produced a kind of backlash, and has prompted some scientists to argue, 'Perhaps we *are* alone in the universe'. Dr Frank Tipler, the best-known exponent of this view, has given one of his papers the provocative title, 'There Are No Intelligent Extra-Terrestrials'. Dr Carl Sagan and his school argue (and I agree with them) that it is much too early to jump to such far-reaching conclusions.

Meanwhile the controversy rages; as has been well said, *either* answer will be awe-inspiring. The question can only be settled by evidence, not by any amount of logic, however plausible. I would like to see the whole debate given a rest while the radio-astronomers, like goldminers panning for gold dust, quietly sieve through the torrents

The peaceful farmlands of southern England are the setting for the latest mystery to intrigue UFO investigators: more a case of 'What are they?' than 'Where are they?'. Every summer since 1980, huge and apparently perfect circles of flattened corn have been found in the midst of otherwise undisturbed crops. A cluster at Cheesefoot Head, Hampshire, in 1986 (*top left*) included bizarre double rings (*below left*). At Goodworth Common in the same county the circles were laid out in neat formation (*top right*), and the corn

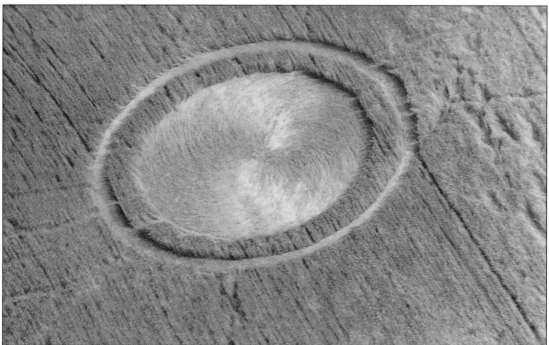

stalks appeared to have been beaten down in a precise clockwise pattern.

Many UFO buffs believe they are the tracks or overnight 'nests' of alien spacecraft, but one leading meteorologist argues that the circles are made by a rare phenomenon known as a 'fair weather stationary whirlwind'. This occurs when a whirlwind becomes trapped in one particular spot by a hill or escarpment. Some whirlwinds have several vortices, hence the 'clusters'.

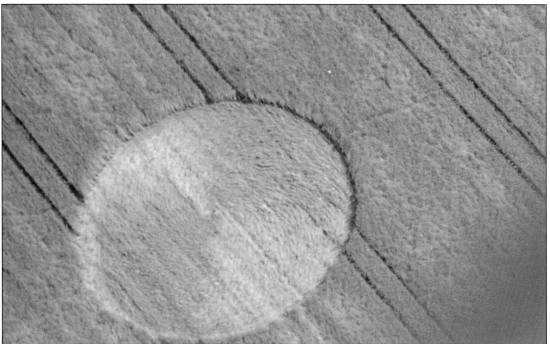

of noise pouring down from the sky.

There is another – and much more speculative – line of approach to this problem. Let me give an analogy to explain what I mean. If a visiting traveller had surveyed our planet from space 10,000 years ago, he would have seen many signs of life – forests, grasslands, great herds of animals – but no trace of intelligence. Today, even a casual glance would reveal cities, roads, airfields, irrigation systems – and, at night, vast constellations of artificial light. (Incidentally, you'll never guess where the most conspicuous of those displays are to be found. The people who operate the military reconnaissance satellites were amazed to find that enormous areas of the Pacific Ocean are brighter than London or New York. You can blame the Japanese fishing fleets: they're pouring megawatts of light into the sea to attract squids – and doing heaven knows what to the local ecology in the process.) These 'advertisements' of terrestrial civilization would have been beyond the imagination of our Stone Age ancestors. Can one set any limits to what might be achieved by a really advanced, long-lived society, with thousands of centuries of space-faring behind it? In particular, might it not have – literally – set its sign among the stars, as we have done upon the earth? As long ago as 1929 the physicist, J. D. Bernal, in one of the most daring works of scientific imagination ever penned, wrote:

> It is unlikely that man will stop until he has roamed over and colonized most of the sidereal universe, or that even this will be the end. Man will not ultimately be content to be parasitic on the stars but will invade them and organize them for his own purpose ... By intelligent organization the life of the universe could probably be prolonged many millions of millions of times ...

Later writers have talked about the 'Greening of the Galaxy', and asked why the stellar sky is so untidy and badly organized ... Where, indeed, are the cosmic engineers?

Perhaps – like ants crawling around the base of the Empire State Building – we simply haven't recognized what's going on all about us. During the last few decades, astronomers have been discovering some very strange phenomena in space, and have been straining scientific theories to the limit in attempts to find *natural* explanations.

Pulsars were the first example. In 1967, when Hewish and Bell discovered radio sources ticking away more accurately than any mechanical clock ever made by man, their first wild speculation was that they might be artificial. Indeed, no astronomer before 1920 could have explained how Mother Nature could have contrived such a prodigy unaided. Well, we are now quite sure that pulsars are indeed natural (though amazing) objects – tiny dying stars acting like cosmic beacons as they spin madly on their axes. But there are other phenomena not so readily explained, and I should not be in the least surprised if the astronomers finally give up on them and admit: 'We're sure that nature can't be responsible. Somebody out there has forgotten to switch off the lights.' Or worse. The most chilling explanation I have heard of one titanic outpouring of cosmic energies is: an industrial accident.

Nowadays, anyone who considers that alien super-civilizations may exist has to contend not with scepticism but with something much worse – credulity. Although the subject now affects me with uncontrollable fits of yawning, I would be failing in my duty if I did not say something about UFOs. So here, as briefly as possible, are the conclusions I've come to after more than fifty years of study (fifty-seven, to be exact, since I first read Charles Fort's *Lo!* in 1930: that monument of eccentric scholarship, published long before anyone had ever heard of 'Flying Saucers', listed apparent celestial visitations right back to the Middle Ages):

1. There may be strange and surprising meteorological, electrical or astronomical phenomena still unknown to science, which may account for the very few UFOs that are both genuine and unexplained.

2. There is no hard evidence that earth has *ever* been visited from space.

3. If that *does* happen, there are at least three independent global radar networks that will know within a matter of minutes. And, in the unlikely event that the US, USSR and Chinese authorities instantly cooperate to suppress the news, they'll succeed for a maximum of forty-eight hours. How long do you imagine such a secret could be kept? Remember how quickly Watergate unravelled . . .

I'd like to add one further item in support of the above. A friend of mine, who (before he was promoted to a much bigger job) was Deputy Director of the CIA, once told me a very interesting story. On his first day with the Company, he called together his top scientists – and the CIA has some of the best – and said to them: 'Come clean with me, boys. What's the truth about this UFO business?'

And they gave him the two answers which I've given everyone for years – and which virtually all scientists who have studied the problem now accept:

1. We all think that there's probably a lot of life – and intelligence – out there among the stars.

2. There's not the slightest firm evidence that it's ever come here . . .

Having written thousands of words on the subject (and read millions), I refuse to go into further details. If anybody wants to argue, I'll merely quote one of my favourite book titles: *Shut up, he explained.*

Finally, if 'they' are out there, what do they look like? I suggest you go to the local zoo and take your choice. Nature tries everything at least once – and has lots of time and space for experimenting. But I will tell you what they will *not* look like. We now understand the principles, if not the details, of human evolution. We specimens of *H. sapiens* are the product of thousands of successive throws of the genetic dice – any one of which might have turned out differently. If the terrestrial experiment started all over again at Time Zero, there might still be intelligence on this planet – but it wouldn't look like us. In the dance of the DNA spirals, the same partners would never meet again. As Loren Eisley wrote thirty years ago in *The Immense Journey*:

> Nowhere in all space or on a thousand worlds will there be men to share our loneliness. There may be wisdom; there may be power; somewhere across space great instruments . . . may stare vainly at our floating cloud wrack, their owners yearning as we yearn. Nevertheless, in the nature of life and in the principles of evolution we have had our answer. Of men elsewhere, and beyond, there will be none forever.

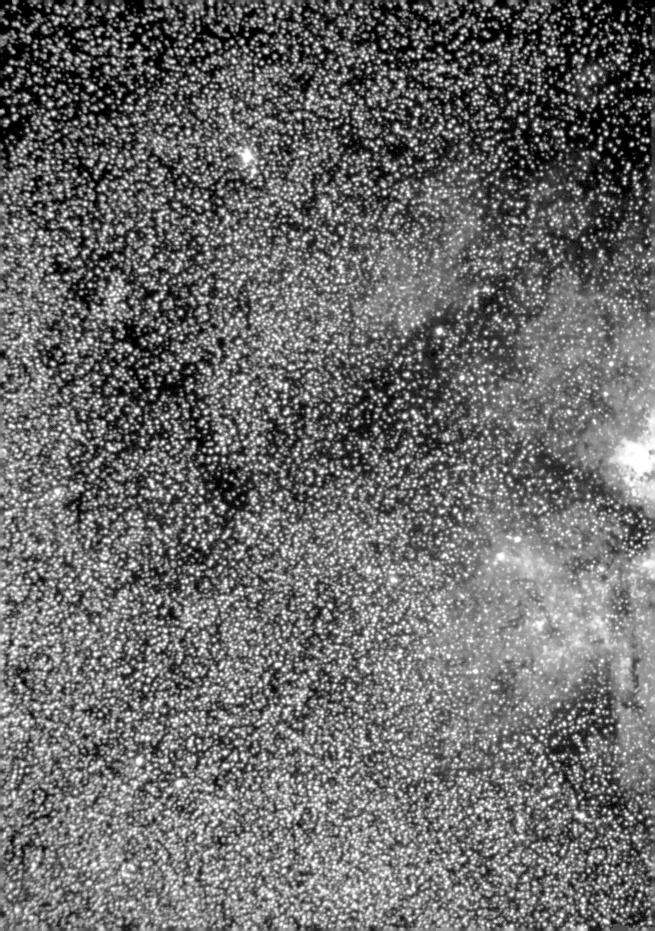

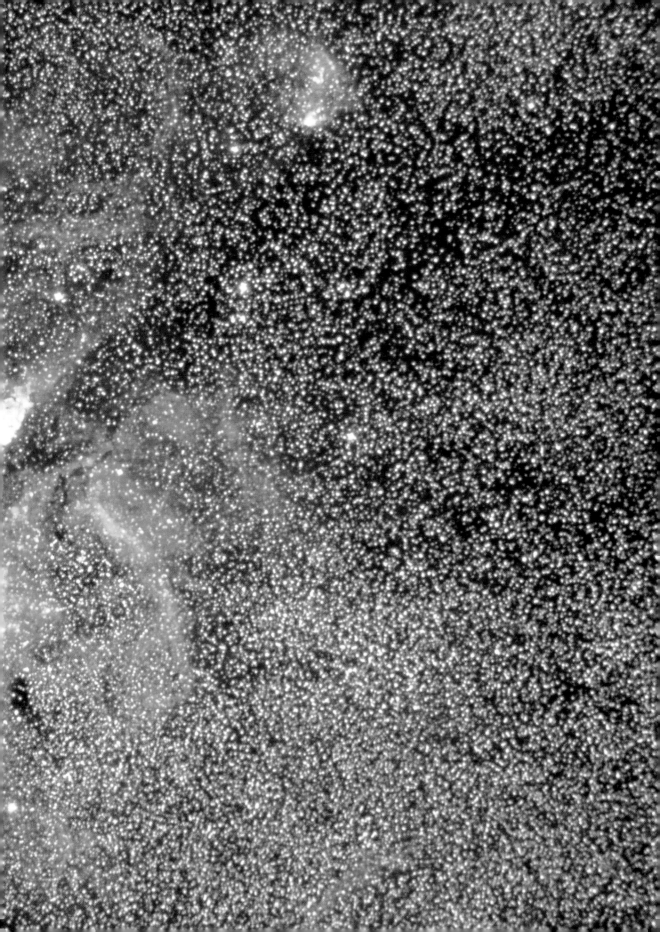

Acknowledgments

Mysteries seem to stimulate letter writers. Like Arthur C. Clarke we have received letters from all over the world from viewers of the *Mysterious World* and *Strange Powers* television series and readers of the accompanying books. (Our postbag on the day that these acknowledgments are being written brought some fascinating observations from a locksmith in Picton, Canada, on some psychokinesis experiments featured in *Strange Powers*, and another correspondent sent us this gem of parapsychological philosophy from Mr Woody Allen: 'Of course there is an unseen world. The only questions are: how far is it from midtown, and how late does it stay open?') Invariably, those who have written to us have cast light upon the mysteries we have examined, some offering first-hand experience, others well-argued theories. Many have suggested new lines of inquiry. We are grateful to all our correspondents, many of whom are mentioned in the text.

In following new developments in research and thinking we have found several publications both enjoyable and indispensable: *Archaeology, Fortean Times*, the *Journal* of the Society for Psychical Research, the *Skeptical Inquirer*, and the *Newsletter* and *Journal* of the International Society of Cryptozoology. We also thank the librarians at Aberdeen University, the London Library, the Harry Price Library and Yorkshire Television who have tracked down the many rare volumes we have used in our researches.

Melvin Harris not only undertook the picture research for this book but has also enthusiastically allowed us to draw upon his vast knowledge of all things apparently mysterious. We are grateful, too, to our colleagues who worked with us on the *Mysterious World* and *Strange Powers* television series, and to Arthur C. Clarke's associates in both Sri Lanka and Somerset for their help.

Above all, we thank our friend Arthur C. Clarke, whose tale of a sea monster narrated on a rock on the beach at Unawatuna brought the Mysterious World into being.

JOHN FAIRLEY
SIMON WELFARE

Photo Credits

166   Mary Evans Picture Library
168–169   B. & C. Alexander
170   Mary Evans Picture Library
171   Media Research
172   Anthony Jay/Group Two Photography
175   John Freeman & Co.
176   Melvin Harris
177   Mary Evans Picture Library
178   Colin Andrews
179   (above) Taylor
179   (below) Colin Andrews
182–183   Smithsonian Institution
Maps by Brian Lloyd

Index